119568855

THE
PALACE OF
VERSAILLES

THE PALACE OF VERSAILLES

by James Barter

Lucent Books, Inc., San Diego, California

Library of Congress Cataloging-in-Publication Data

Barter, James, 1946–
    The Palace of Versailles / by James Barter.
        p.   cm. — (Building history series)
    Includes bibliographical references and index.
    Summary: Describes the building of the extravagant palace
at Versailles in its historical context, particularly as a reflection
of the personality and influence of Louis XIV.
    ISBN 1-56006-433-1 (lib. : alk. paper)
    1. Château de Versailles (Versailles, France)—History—Juvenile
literature.   2. Versailles (France)—Buildings, structures, etc.—
Juvenile literature.   3. Louis XIV, King of France, 1638–1715—
Influence—Juvenile literature.   4. Gardens—France—Versailles
—Juvenile literature.   5. France—Court and courtiers—Juvenile
literature.   [1. Versailles (France)—Buildings, structures, etc.
2. Louis XIV, King of France, 1638–1715.   3. Palaces—France.
4. France—History—16th century.   5. France—History—17th
century.]   I. Title.   II. Series
DC801.V57B35   1999
944'.366—dc21   98-15262
                                                                      CIP
                                                                       AC

Copyright 1999 by Lucent Books, Inc.
P.O. Box 289011, San Diego, California, 92198-9011

Printed in the U.S.A.

CONTENTS

FOREWORD

Throughout history, as civilizations have evolved and prospered, each has produced unique buildings and architectural styles. Combining the need for both utility and artistic expression, a society's buildings, particularly its large-scale public structures, often reflect the individual character traits that distinguish it from other societies. In a very real sense, then, buildings express a society's values and unique characteristics in tangible form. As scholar Anita Abramovitz comments in her book *People and Spaces*, "Our ways of living and thinking—our habits, needs, fear of enemies, aspirations, materialistic concerns, and religious beliefs—have influenced the kinds of spaces that we build and that later surround and include us."

That specific types and styles of structures constitute an outward expression of the spirit of an individual people or era can be seen in the diverse ways that various societies have built palaces, fortresses, tombs, churches, government buildings, sports arenas, public works, and other such monuments. The ancient Greeks, for instance, were a supremely rational people who originated Western philosophy and science, including the atomic theory and the realization that the earth is a sphere. Their public buildings, epitomized by Athens's magnificent Parthenon temple, were equally rational, emphasizing order, harmony, reason, and above all, restraint.

By contrast, the Romans, who conquered and absorbed the Greek lands, were a highly practical people preoccupied with acquiring and wielding power over others. The Romans greatly admired and readily copied elements of Greek architecture, but modified and adapted them to their own needs. "Roman genius was called into action by the enormous practical needs of a world empire," wrote historian Edith Hamilton. "Rome met them magnificently. Buildings tremendous, indomitable, amphitheaters where eighty thousand could watch a spectacle, baths where three thousand could bathe at the same time."

In medieval Europe, God heavily influenced and motivated the people, and religion permeated all aspects of society, molding people's worldviews and guiding their everyday actions. That spiritual mindset is reflected in the most important medieval structure—the Gothic cathedral—which, in a sense, was a model of heavenly cities. As scholar Anne Fremantle so elegantly phrases it, the cathedrals were "harmonious elevations of stone and glass reaching up to heaven to seek and receive the light [of God]."

Our more secular modern age, in contrast, is driven by the realities of a global economy, advanced technology, and mass communications. Responding to the needs of international trade and the growth of cities housing millions of people, today's builders construct engineering marvels, among them towering skyscrapers of steel and glass, mammoth marine canals, and huge and elaborate rapid transit systems, all of which would have left their ancestors, even the Romans, awestruck.

In examining some of humanity's greatest edifices, Lucent Books' Building History series recognizes this close relationship between a society's historical character and its buildings. Each volume in the series begins with a historical sketch of the people who erected the edifice, exploring their major achievements as well as the beliefs, customs, and societal needs that dictated the variety, functions, and styles of their buildings. A detailed explanation of how the selected structure was conceived, designed, and built, to the extent that this information is known, makes up the majority of the volume.

Each volume in the Lucent Building History series also includes several special features that are useful tools for additional research. A chronology of important dates gives students an overview, at a glance, of the evolution and use of the structure described. Sidebars create a broader context by adding further details on some of the architects, engineers, and construction tools, materials, and methods that made each structure a reality, as well as the social, political, and/or religious leaders and movements that inspired its creation. Useful maps help the reader locate the nations, cities, streets, and individual structures mentioned in the text; and numerous diagrams and pictures illustrate tools and devices that bring to life various stages of construction. Finally, each volume contains two bibliographies, one for student research, the other listing works the author consulted in compiling the book.

Taken as a whole, these volumes, covering diverse ancient and modern structures, constitute not only a valuable research tool, but also a tribute to the human spirit, a fascinating exploration of the dreams, skills, ingenuity, and dogged determination of the great peoples who shaped history.

Important Dates in the Building of the Palace of Versailles

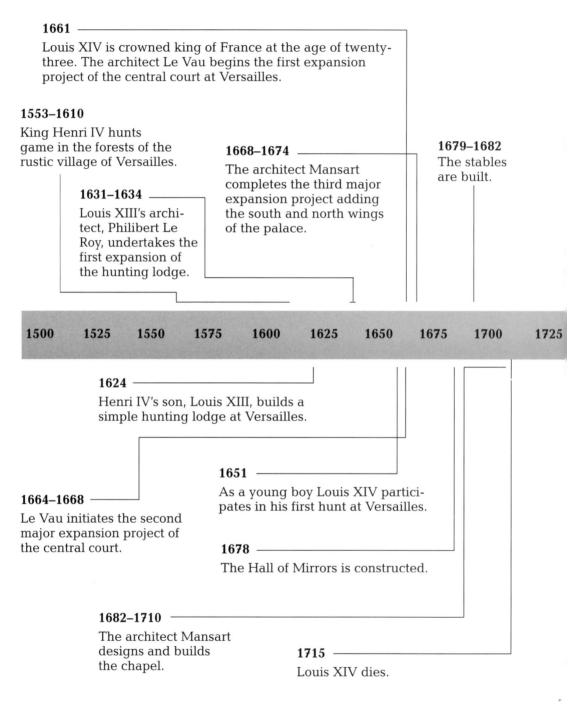

1661

Louis XIV is crowned king of France at the age of twenty-three. The architect Le Vau begins the first expansion project of the central court at Versailles.

1553–1610

King Henri IV hunts game in the forests of the rustic village of Versailles.

1631–1634

Louis XIII's architect, Philibert Le Roy, undertakes the first expansion of the hunting lodge.

1668–1674

The architect Mansart completes the third major expansion project adding the south and north wings of the palace.

1679–1682

The stables are built.

| 1500 | 1525 | 1550 | 1575 | 1600 | 1625 | 1650 | 1675 | 1700 | 1725 |

1624

Henri IV's son, Louis XIII, builds a simple hunting lodge at Versailles.

1651

As a young boy Louis XIV participates in his first hunt at Versailles.

1664–1668

Le Vau initiates the second major expansion project of the central court.

1678

The Hall of Mirrors is constructed.

1682–1710

The architect Mansart designs and builds the chapel.

1715

Louis XIV dies.

The magnificent Palace of Versailles, home to French nobility of the seventeenth and eighteenth centuries.

1789
The French Revolution begins. Mobs storm Versailles, and Louis XVI and the court are forced to flee.

1919
The Treaty of Versailles ending World War I is signed in the Hall of Mirrors.

1962
French president Charles De Gaulle initiates the restoration of the Large Trianon.

1833–1837
Versailles is transformed into a museum.

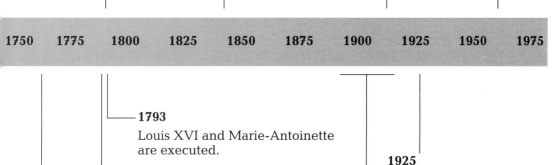

1750   1775   1800   1825   1850   1875   1900   1925   1950   1975

1793
Louis XVI and Marie-Antoinette are executed.

1925
Versailles receives a Rockefeller Grant for further restoration.

1783–1785
Louis XVI has the Hamlet built for his queen, Marie-Antoinette.

1762
Louis XV orders construction of Small Trianon to begin.

1892–1920
The central palace undergoes extensive restoration.

Introduction

Ever since the seventeenth-century reign of King Louis XIV of France, between 1643 and 1715, people throughout the world have associated the Palace of Versailles with the most extravagant example of self-indulgent living. All kings of that era viewed their palaces as status symbols, and none had more status than did Louis. The fame of his palace and elaborate gardens at Versailles spread throughout the continent, attracting kings and queens as guests who returned home overwhelmed by the unprecedented size and opulence of the palace they had visited.

The Extravagance of a King

Part royal pleasure palace, part theme park, part French court, and part prison, the international fame of this estate was not due to innovative architectural or engineering features but rather to its size. Set on 19,262 acres of elegant picturesque gardens and hunting grounds, the entire estate was larger than both modern day Paris and the island of Manhattan in New York. The five thousand French nobles required to live on the estate as Louis's guests idly passed their time in lavish surroundings. Both guests and the estate were cared for and protected by seven thousand servants, four thousand Swiss and French foot guards, and another four thousand guards on horseback. Attractive as this may seem, the nobles could not leave without the permission of the king. Louis kept them under his watchful eye to prevent them from interfering with his autocratic rule.

To accommodate the nobles and to prevent them from escaping back to their own homes throughout France was an expensive undertaking. Louis continually expanded the main palace until it became nearly a half-mile long, and later built additional palaces on the estate. The main palace contained 1,852 individual apartments, 1,252 fireplaces, 2,143 windows, and stables for two thousand royal horses. Maintenance at the palace required an endless number of service rooms for preparing food, cleaning and heating the palace, making and cleaning clothes, stabling the thousands of horses, storing goods and materials, and entertaining the nobility.

Official accounts maintained throughout construction of the palace and its many gardens record a staggering financial drain on the economy of 116,438,892 livres. The historian James

Farmer estimated this amount to be equivalent to $100 million when he published his book in 1905. To place this amount in current terms brings the cost to about $2 billion, far more expensive than any modern luxury hotel and more than all but the largest theme parks. These financial accounts do not record the cost to human life, although literary references record hundreds of workers dying of illness, from being buried alive in mud, and from being trampled to death by the thousands of draft horses used to haul mud and debris during construction.

What had begun during the reign of Louis's father, Louis XIII (1601–1643), as a rustic hunting lodge for a few close friends, evolved into a grandiose manifestation of unbridled aristocratic extravagance under Louis XIV, Louis XV, and Louis XVI. The Palace of Versailles encompassed limitless marble corridors and sweeping staircases, miles of walks in sculptured gardens, quantities of gold leaf furniture, hallways and rooms filled with art, Epicurean feasts, music, theater, and the perversities of court intrigue.

In 1643, at the age of five, Louis XIV ascended to the French throne following the death of his father, Louis XIII. Later crowned King of France in 1661 when he was twenty-three, Louis lived at the time of a new political mandate called absolutism. This mandate, spreading over much of Europe at this

The Palace of Versailles was a symbol of King Louis XIV's status. It contained extravagant gardens, hunting grounds, and stables large enough to house two thousand horses.

time, had as its premise the belief that supreme power of government belonged in the hands of one absolute ruler. Of all the absolute rulers of Europe, Louis XIV was the best known and the most extreme example. Unchecked by an elected legislature or court system, Louis indulged his desires for an extravagant lifestyle and military conquest. It was Louis who made the comment "L'état, c'est moi," "I am the state." Louis went even further during his reign, believing that God had wished him to reign as king over all the French people and declared himself to be "Le Roi Soleil," "The Sun King." It never occurred to Louis to not build the largest and most expensive estate in Europe, and he never doubted that he could do it; his power was absolute. The Palace of Versailles was the grand extravagance that will forever be associated with his reign.

King Louis XIV believed he was divinely chosen to rule France. Declaring his absolute power, Louis proclaimed himself "Le Roi Soleil," "The Sun King."

The historical significance of Versailles divides contemporary historians into two camps. One camp views Versailles as having little historical significance, representing nothing more than the extravagance of the king. Versailles, they believe, represents the unrestrained whim of an autocratic ruler who squandered the wealth of France on personal pleasure. The other camp views Versailles as an important historical manifestation of this period. This camp believes that the study of Versailles reveals insight not only into the administration of France at this time but, more importantly, into the genesis of the French Revolution of 1789.

The
Hunting Lodge

Before it became famous for having the world's largest and most luxurious palace, Versailles was a small rural hamlet ten miles southwest of Paris in the midst of small plots of land tilled by peasant farmers. The major road from Paris to the coastal towns along the Atlantic Ocean ran through Versailles, nonetheless bringing barely enough visitors to fill three small rustic inns. Several streams and ponds saturated Versailles's long Galie valley, creating a marshy environment suited for little but grazing cattle and harboring the local game animals of deer, fox, geese, wild boar, and rabbits.

Unsuitable for large-scale cultivation, this valley became a popular hunting preserve for the French kings in the early 1500s. King Henri IV (1553–1610), ruler of France from 1589 to 1610, and his noble friends enjoyed spending most of their days in this valley hunting from horseback. His son, King Louis XIII, first hunted here with his father when he was only six.

The Hunting Lodge

After a long day's hunt, the late night ride back to Paris became an annoyance to Louis and his hunting party. In 1623, he built a small, modest lodge at Versailles where he and his friends could spend the night before returning to Paris the next morning. This initial hunting lodge had nothing more than a few private

THE HUNT

To the nobility, the hunt was more than merely chasing and shooting animals. It was a lifestyle reserved for the very rich, providing the nobility with an opportunity to practice the art of warfare on horseback. During the hunt, the nobility practiced military tactics that required great skill, such as charging through thick brush, storming across streams, and shooting or stabbing their quarry from the saddle.

During a hunt, the nobility could practice their military skills by using guns, swords, or daggers to kill game animals. Such excursions sparked Louis XIII to build the modest hunting lodge that would eventually become the great palace.

bedrooms for overnight sleeping. Intended to be nothing more than a lodge for hunters, Louis saw no need to consult an architect for the construction. The site for the lodge, an important consideration, was at the top of a slight rise on the property. This high ground provided the king and his friends a good view of the long Galie valley to the west and a location that would remain dry during the wet winter months.

The lodge consisted of a central building with two wings at right angles to one another forming a horseshoe-shaped structure, with a wall enclosing the fourth side and forming a square. This building had two stories, with the king's apartment on the

The first part of the hunt was the chase. This was fast action filled with quick, exciting maneuvers. Local peasants often climbed to the tops of trees to watch the hunters as they flashed through the brush and woods. Of all the types of game animals, the kings favored the stag. When the stag was cornered, a gun, sword, or dagger killed the animal.

After the hunting party had killed the stag, they brought its carcass to the king, who greeted the hunters and spectators at his balcony. The dogs that had taken part in the chase, lunging at the carcass of the stag, were kept back with whips. With a gesture from the king, the captain of the hounds released them to attack the stag. The dogs tore its flesh from the bones, and then, an attendant cut open the belly of the stag, placed the organs on a long wooden fork, and threw them to the dogs to be devoured. Following this carnage, a fanfare of trumpets sounded, signaling everyone to go home.

A day's hunt for a large number of the king's nobility sometimes wreaked havoc over the countryside farmed by peasants. Hundreds of horses charging after a deer or fox often ran through grain fields, destroying the summer crop before the harvest. Thundering down the many narrow dirt roads crisscrossing the landscape, the riders trampled to death chickens, geese, and ducks raised by the peasants for their eggs and meat. At the end of the day, the peasants who had lost crops or animals returned to their hamlets having possibly lost their entire livelihood for the year.

second floor consisting of four rooms, and a series of much smaller and less comfortable bedrooms for his attendants.

In June of 1624, builders dug a moat around Louis XIII's hunting lodge to prevent unwanted people from disturbing the king. As was the case at Versailles, the moat was often set a short distance away from structures to allow for the placement of cannon for defense of the building.

By then, Louis was visiting Versailles with greater frequency and with larger numbers of friends. It came as no surprise to anyone that he wished for greater comfort and more room. In a short period of time, Louis began purchasing more land in the

Galie valley in anticipation of expanding both his private hunting park and his modest hunting lodge.

EXPANDING THE HUNTING LODGE

A few years after Louis XIII built the hunting lodge he purchased the surrounding 100-acre estate and, in 1632, completed a substantial addition to the original lodge. One year later he added another 150 acres in the Galie valley. With this second addition, it was clear to everyone that Louis had larger plans for this rustic hunting lodge, yet no one could then have guessed just how large those plans would become under his son, Louis XIV.

Louis intended the expansion of 1632 to be more regal than the initial hunting lodge. To achieve his vision, he hired the architect Philibert Le Roy to direct the work. Le Roy, an experienced architect, had designed other large châteaux and understood

King Louis XIII (pictured) started the expansion of the hunting lodge by purchasing the surrounding land and hiring architect Philibert Le Roy.

the engineering required for these large structures. Very few plans or drawings describing the precise engineering of the château have survived. Historians have been able to hypothesize how the château was built, however, by examining detailed notes of other châteaux built by Le Roy and other architects of the time.

Le Roy enlarged the main building, widening it from twenty feet to twenty-six feet. The king's rooms were made more elaborate and Le Roy added a central staircase. He covered the exterior of the lodge with a combination of stone and brick. When workers had completed the renovation, the exterior colors of red brick, white stone, and black slate for the roof created a new style used on future palaces throughout France. Le Roy then added eleven large windows to create a wonderful view of the Galie valley. The total cost for all of Louis's building programs at Versailles was 300,000 livres, a relatively modest price. Of this amount 213,000 paid for the château and 87,000 for the gardens.

SEVENTEENTH-CENTURY CONSTRUCTION METHODS

The construction of palaces, châteaux, and other large homes for the royalty of France was a well-understood craft. Dozens had been built in other parts of France before Louis XIII built at Versailles. Simple in their form and materials, their evolution dated back to the architecture of the Romans, who had once conquered and ruled all of France.

The first job for Le Roy was to determine the type and size of expansion for the king's existing hunting lodge. When this was known, the architect drew exterior views of the building to demonstrate the size, the elevations, and the new rooflines. After the king approved the drawings of the exterior views the architect drew the interior views, showing the rooms, hallways, staircases, fireplaces, kitchens, stables, and general-purpose rooms. If walls or roofs required special engineering for support, he drew detailed plans to assist the builders.

The implementation of the plans began with leveling the expanded site and digging the trenches for the foundation. Peasant workers from the village of Versailles provided the labor. Engineers stretched ropes to outline the foundation trenches and the workers dug the trenches with picks and shovels. While the trenches were being dug, horse-drawn carts hauled stone blocks from nearby limestone quarries for use in the foundation. Masons then cut the stones to precise sizes at the construction site of the new château.

This diagram shows the horseshoe shape of the château with the Marble Court in the center.

The stonemasons set the stone blocks into the trenches, leaving a one-inch space, called a grout line, between each of the blocks. They then filled the grout line with concrete to hold the blocks together. Many layers of stone were stacked until they reached a height a few feet above ground level. Engineers some-times used iron clamps in addition to concrete to prevent the stones from separating. To secure the iron clamps in the stones, stonemasons first drilled holes in the top horizontal plane of each stone. After filling the grout line with concrete, ironworkers set the bracket-shaped iron bars in the holes across the joint line to clamp one block to the next. With the completion of the foundation, the stonemasons began setting the stone and brick exterior walls.

As the walls took shape, carpenters went to the nearby woods to cut trees for scaffold lumber. Scaffolds were quickly built to provide a place for the stonemasons to stand while set-ting stone. As the walls went up, workers left spaces for the later addition of windows.

Although the blocks were not very large, lifting them high off the ground required the use of wooden cranes operated by hand. These cranes, similar in design to those used by the an-

SEVENTEENTH-CENTURY CHÂTEAUX

Before the Palace of Versailles, the kings and nobles of France built châteaux throughout the country. As far back as the twelfth century, châteaux began to dot the French coun-tryside. The term *château* conveys the idea of a large formal home for royalty in the countryside. Larger ones consisted of over one hundred rooms set on several thousand acres of for-mal gardens and hunting forests. Many had stone walls and moats for their defense and a few had drawbridges.

A king's château functioned as a home for the royal fam-ily and a place where the king met with his advisors to make governmental decisions affecting the affairs of the nation. To perform both functions, the design of a château included rooms for the personal use of the king's family as well as rooms for conducting official government business.

The design of a typical two-story château for the royal family focused on a series of rooms called apartments. It was common for the king's apartment to have a suite of as many as six or eight rooms for his own use, a slightly smaller num-ber for the queen, and a smaller number for children.

The rooms used for government business, called salons, were generally located in a separate wing or wings of the château. The function of a salon was to provide a large meet-

cient Romans, had ropes wound around large wheels. As workers turned a wheel, the rope wrapped around it raised the
stones. Workers used wooden devices set on rollers made from
tree trunks to move large stones to the cranes.

FROM HUNTING LODGE TO CHÂTEAU

Modern French historians studying this surge of building under
Louis XIII ask what caused him to expand the rustic hunting
lodge into a more elegant château? Was it more than the wish
for an elaborate hunting lodge or was he simply tired of sleeping in hay mounds? Historians identify many reasons for the expansion project.

Louis did not seem to be a devoted husband or a man who
enjoyed the company of women. Unlike other royal residences,
Versailles purposefully lacked an apartment for Louis's wife,
Queen Anne of Austria. It was clear that this was to be a place

ing area where dignitaries to the king's court gathered to discuss the affairs of the nation with the king.

The king's architects designed and decorated the apartments and salons to display the wealth of the king. Each major room had a large colorful marble fireplace, crystal
chandeliers for lighting, floors made of marble or wood parquet, and ceilings painted with fanciful and colorful scenes
of people and exotic places.

Visiting dignitaries and friends usually traveled many
days on horseback or in carriages. Accommodating all of
them required the usual support rooms. Kitchens, for example, had walk-in fireplaces where whole deer and sides of
beef roasted on rotisseries.

A château also required a large staff of servants and a
large number of rooms for the basic operations of the
château. The servants often received no pay, working instead for food and perhaps a place to sleep. Servants worked
in the kitchens and gardens preparing meals, chopping and
carrying wood to heat the rooms, cleaning the floors and doing laundry, and attending to any other needs of the family
and their royal guests.

of personal retreat for Louis, far from his queen. In 1635, an epidemic of smallpox broke out in Paris. Louis wrote to his advisor, Cardinal Richelieu (1585–1642), suggesting that the royal children might be safer at Versailles, but he went on to say, "I suppose that the queen could be lodged at Versailles with my children but I fear her group of female friends whose presence here would spoil everything for me."

At this same time, Louis met a woman by the name of Louise de La Layette, whom he found more attractive than the queen. He agreed to allow her to reside at Versailles and, according to the memoirs of Madame de Motteville, a resident at the palace writing in 1723, "Louis allowed her to reside at Versailles, subject to his orders and at his disposal. The young woman however was not the least interested in Louis and, escaping his advances, she entered a convent."

Louis XIII's wife, Queen Anne of Austria. Louis did not want Anne to reside at Versailles, fearing that her presence would ruin the atmosphere at his fraternal lodge.

The modern French architect and historian Pierre-André Lablaude suggests that, in addition to these reasons for the building project, another reason may have influenced the expansion. Louis XIII had first hunted at Versailles with his father at the age of six. Lablaude proposes that fond memories of Louis's early hunting days with his father may have justified additional financial investment in Versailles.

LOUIS XIII'S PLACE IN HISTORY

Historians find no evidence suggesting that, beyond ordering them, Louis was actively involved in any of the building programs at Versailles. The palace as it stands today, the largest and most elegant one ever built, is the result of Louis's son, Louis XIV. At the time of Louis XIII's death, however, the lodge remained nothing more than a personal hunting retreat for the king, and there is no evidence that Louis ever intended it to be used for family or government purposes.

As the king of France, Louis XIII was no more involved in determining the politics of his country than in building his château at Versailles. Although he ruled for thirty-three years,

Louis XIII is not highly regarded as a king by historians. For the first fifteen years of his reign, France floundered under the supervision of Louis's mother, Marie de Médicis. In 1624, when Louis was twenty-three years old, his advisors pressured him to choose as his most trusted advisor a cardinal in the Roman Catholic Church named Richelieu (1585–1642). Historians tend to point out only two important events in Louis's life: the birth of his far more significant son, Louis XIV, and the appointment of his chief advisor, Cardinal Richelieu.

Chief advisors such as Richelieu who ruled in place of kings were common throughout many of the royal families of sixteenth- and seventeenth-century Europe. When historians explain this phenomenon, they do so by looking at the social order of peasants and nobility.

PEASANTRY AND NOBILITY

Life four hundred years ago in France when Versailles was still a small rural town was unlike anything imaginable in France or America today. Versailles and all other towns throughout France, large and small, were emerging from a thousand-year-old custom of dividing all people into two social groups based on heredity: the peasantry and the nobility.

The peasantry was a class of people primarily tied to the land as poor farmers or to small shops as merchants. This group had two primary responsibilities: to raise crops or create goods and to pay most of the taxes needed to support the government. A few owned their own land, and a small middle class of merchants was developing, but most farmed the land owned by the wealthier nobility. Hard work, long days, and a poor diet made many of them old by the time they were forty. Demands on the peasants by the nobility were sometimes unreasonable, but there were no courts to address the peasants' complaints. Forced to work hard for low wages, peasants had few rights and little hope of escaping their life of poverty. These people provided the cheap labor needed to construct Louis's château.

The lives of the peasants rarely changed. Born peasants, they could do little to lift themselves out of poverty. The class system prevented peasants from marrying outside of their class, from moving to different parts of the country, from acquiring an education, from pursuing jobs other than those of their parents, and from having access to law courts. Historians have documented

CARDINAL RICHELIEU

Richelieu provided the much-needed leadership of France until his death in 1642, eighteen years after his appointment to office. Acting in place of the king for all important decisions, Richelieu had two primary objectives: to destroy all of the nobility opposing Louis and to wage war against other European powers that threatened France's position in Europe.

Richelieu, by vigorous and effective measures, succeeded in breaking the political power of the great families of France, making the king an absolute ruler. Richelieu executed several members of the nobility who opposed the absolute power of the king, destroyed their châteaux, and confiscated their possessions.

To establish France as the dominant power in Europe, Richelieu sought to destroy France's principal enemy, Austria. To accomplish this, he gave France's support to the enemies of Austria's Habsburg Empire during the Thirty Years' War (1618–1648). During this war (actually a series of wars), France's military

Cardinal Richelieu, advisor to Louis XIII, made all the major decisions that ensured France's dominance in Europe.

contribution was minimal; instead Richelieu gave Sweden money to carry on the fight against the Habsburgs while France was winning its own war with Spain over the disputed territory of Mantua. Because France did not share in the devastation wrought by the Thirty Years' War, France emerged at war's end as a strong nation. Though Richelieu did not live to see France's triumph over Austria and Spain, his plan to ensure his nation's dominance in Europe succeeded.

Richelieu was the one man who did more to shape France during Louis XIII's reign than did Louis himself. This circumstance, where the king assumed little responsibility for ruling the country, instead allowing an advisor to make all major decisions, was not new to France or the continent. Advisors who ruled in place of kings were common throughout many of the royal families of sixteenth- and seventeenth-century Europe.

the peasants' desire to break out of poverty as well as the nobility's refusal to allow them to do so.

The French nobility was a class of about twelve hundred aristocratic families who controlled most of the land and wealth of France. This group had two primary responsibilities: to assist the king in the administration of the country and to lead the army into war. The number of these families was not large, but generation after generation, they retained their power and wealth.

The kings of France, as well as those of other European countries, had allowed the nobility to assist in making important political, military, and financial decisions. In time, these advisors believed that they had a right to assume these roles, a right to accumulate great sums of money in the process, and the right to make all the important decisions, rendering the king a ruler in name only.

After witnessing several generations of advisors ruling in place of the king, the nobility came to assume that all future kings would also relinquish their royal decision making authority in favor of spending their lives hunting and hosting extravagant parties and state dinners.

The life of a peasant was a continuous cycle of poverty. Although peasants wished to enrich their lives, they remained indentured to the nobility.

THE ASCENDANCY OF LOUIS XIV

The death of Louis XIII in 1643 and the succession of his more assertive son, Louis XIV, mark a significant shift in the history of France. France emerged as the dominant European nation under Louis's firm control. Unlike his father, Louis XIV took command of the government, isolated and subdued the nobility at Versailles, and involved himself directly in all foreign and domestic policies. Of equal importance to Louis XIV was the expansion of the château at Versailles into a palace befitting the image and prestige of the most powerful king in Europe.

When Louis XIV came to the throne at the age of five in 1643, it was only natural that an advisor would be appointed to attend to the affairs of state. Louis's mother chose Cardinal Mazarin to guide the state, just as Richelieu had guided France for Louis XIII. This continuation of the tradition of allowing aristocrats to rule in place of the king was successful until the death of Mazarin in 1660, when Louis XIV was twenty-two years old. One year later,

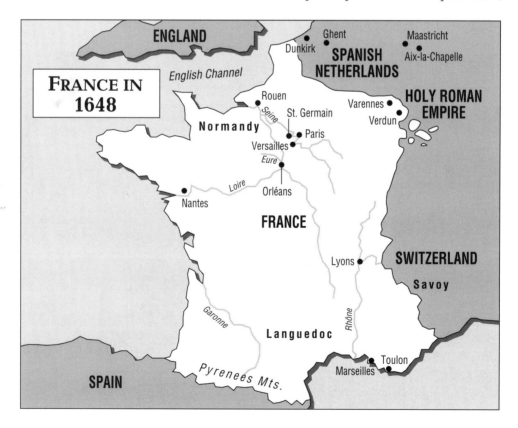

when French nobility awaited his announcement of the new advisor to govern the country, the archbishop of Rouen visited Louis and asked, "To whom shall we address ourselves in the future?" Louis replied, "To me." In Louis's memoirs he later wrote, "It was the moment I had waited for and the moment I dreaded." Louis had decided to rule France.

This famous statement of independence, freeing the king from royal advisors, devastated the nobles hoping to gain access to powerful court positions. This did not mean that Louis XIV would not have advisors to assist him; he frequently did. What it did mean, however, was that for the first time in hundreds of years, many of the king's advisors would no longer be from the ranks of the nobility. Louis's most important advisor, his minister of finances, Jean Baptiste Colbert (1619–1683), was one extremely competent minister who was not from their ranks.

King Louis XIV was the first king in centuries to rule without the aid of advisors from the nobility. Instead, Louis hired more qualified advisors from the middle class.

Could Louis expect the nobility to suddenly change their attitude toward the king's position? Not at all, and for that reason, Louis politely dismissed them from their administrative responsibilities and selected in their place well-qualified advisors, not from the nobility, but rather from the emerging middle class. The middle-class advisors Louis chose were educated people from various backgrounds. Most occupied what historians call the new merchant class, referring to middle-class owners of businesses and members of professional groups such as teachers, lawyers, accountants, and architects.

Could Louis expect the nobility to go back to their estates throughout France without resisting this radical change? Not at all, and for that reason, Louis embarked on a building program dramatically expanding the apartments at Versailles to accommodate the nobility. Louis reasoned that keeping them at Versailles under his watchful eye would be a major expense, but a necessary one.

The Royal Apartments of Louis XIV

Louis XIV had four passions in life: participating in the hunt, finding a new mistress, waging war, and building at Versailles. Of the four, hunting was the only constant activity, with the other three tending to occur in ten-year cycles. Louis found a new mistress each cycle, while waging war and building at Versailles alternated with every other cycle. A review of official records documenting spending on Versailles reveals a pattern of light spending during times of war followed by heavy spending during times of peace. When at war, France's treasury paid for soldiers, cannon, and gunpowder. When at peace, it paid for builders, stone blocks, and cement.

Louis played an active role building Versailles and relished his reputation as a builder, but no activity piqued his interest more than that of war. In an often-quoted letter of September 20, 1663, Jean Baptiste Colbert, Louis's minister of finance, addressed war and building and admonished Louis to complete the Louvre, the king's palace in Paris,

> during the time that [Your Majesty] has spent such large sums of money for this building [Versailles], [Your Majesty] has neglected the Louvre, which is assuredly the finest building in the world, and the most fitting for the grandeur of Your Majesty. Your Majesty is well aware that, except for brilliant military campaigns, nothing signals the grandeur and intelligence of princes more notably than buildings. Posterity judges princes in accordance with the splendor of the residences constructed by them during their reigns. O what a pity if the greatest and most virtuous king were measured by the standard of Versailles! And yet there is no reason to fear this misfortune.

FROM CHÂTEAU TO PALACE

Neither Louis nor his architects drew up a detailed grand design that served as a master plan for Versailles. Instead, Louis surveyed the start of each building project to determine what was required, what needed changing, and what suited his whimsy. For the man who ruled by absolute right and divine right, any project he ordered undertaken was completed as directed. In seventeenth-century France, the king's word was law.

Louis's highest building priority between 1664 and 1668 was the expansion and embellishment of the existing square horseshoe-shaped château built by his father. Advisors had recommended to the king that he should tear down his father's original château and build a new, more elaborate one. Louis, however, faithful to the memory of his father, chose to leave the original building intact but to expand and embellish it. Louis added a new balcony,

Jean Baptiste Colbert, minister of finance for Louis XIV, encouraged the king to forget Versailles and focus his energy on building the Louvre palace.

transformed the existing apartments into elegant rooms filled with art, and enlarged the main entry to the château.

Between 1668 and 1674 the second phase of work, known as the *Enveloppe*, proceeded. The *Enveloppe* derives its name from the plan to envelop the small original château, built by Louis XIII, within the new and more majestic one for Louis XIV. To accomplish this feat, the architect Le Vau extended the walls of the original château to the north, south, and west. The expansion of these wings enlarged the château of Louis XIII by a factor of four. In addition to the expansion of the walls, Le Vau increased the height to three stories, ordered the roof flattened, and directed the entire redecoration of the interior.

This new château continued to expand over time until Louis ordered the addition of north and south wings to accommodate the thousands of residents living there. While the château began to evolve in size and opulence to a true palace, the *Enveloppe* remained the center of courtly life because it was here that the king and queen maintained their fabled royal apartments.

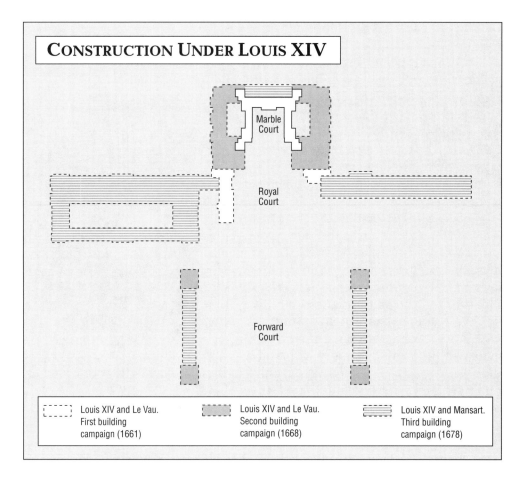

CONSTRUCTION UNDER LOUIS XIV

Marble Court

Royal Court

Forward Court

Louis XIV and Le Vau.
First building
campaign (1661)

Louis XIV and Le Vau.
Second building
campaign (1668)

Louis XIV and Mansart.
Third building
campaign (1678)

THE KING'S APARTMENT

The duties of the king were sufficiently complex to require space to care for his personal needs as well as those of his kingdom. As king, he was commander of the army, the exclusive lawgiver, and controller of the finances for the entire nation. His absolute authority made him a much sought after man. For this reason, the hundreds of members of the court who sought various personal favors from him, along with his advisors and ministers who had legitimate reasons for his time, had to be effectively and efficiently controlled. The various rooms in the suite that made up the king's apartment accomplished this objective.

The rooms of the king's apartment changed over time from the original four under Louis XIV to a different set of seven under Louis XV and XVI. In addition to these seven private rooms,

STRUCTURAL ENGINEERING

Construction of a palace the size of Versailles necessitated more than aesthetic considerations. Failure to adequately support and reinforce the walls and the heavy slate roof would buckle walls, sending the entire structure crashing to the ground. Safety for the king and his court was a constant concern for the royal architects and engineers. Key considerations for safety were proper structural materials and sound engineering techniques.

The foundation of the exterior walls of the palace, which supported most of the weight of the roof, were made of heavy limestone blocks quarried in France. These hand-carved blocks ran from below grade to four feet above grade along most of the perimeter, except at the corners where they rose to the roofline. Above the limestone blocks, stonemasons set standard red paving bricks to complete the walls.

The many exterior windows needed to illuminate the long interior halls during the day presented engineers with unique problems. The windows, unlike the solid walls, lacked the strength to support the roof sections above them. To relieve the weight, engineers designed limestone frames within which the windows were set. The limestone blocks above the windows transferred the weight of the roof above the windows to the vertical supports of the stone frame down to the foundation stones.

Columns, an attractive architectural highlight harkening back to the style of the Greeks and Romans, were widely used at Versailles. Typically, designers placed them at major entrances and in areas of high visibility. Made of solid marble and carved in all three of the classical orders, Doric, Ionic, and Corinthian, columns were capable of supporting tremendous weight. To ensure that they would not collapse, engineers carved each one from a single block of marble and inserted a thick iron rod through a hole bored down the center. This rod ran from the base, through the column shaft, through the capital and was imbedded into the architrave above the capital.

another six rooms were added for official diplomatic meetings, bringing the total used by the kings to an unprecedented thirteen. The original four under Louis XIV are the best known and best preserved.

Access to these second-story apartments was by way of the King's Stairway. Unlike the rooms that made up the royal apartment of the queen, those of the king were interior rooms without views of the sculpture gardens. Although these rooms constituted the private apartment of the king, he rarely had the privacy to enjoy them without the hundreds of aides attending to his needs, advisors requesting his approval for various projects, and nobles seeking his social favors.

The extravagance of the king's apartments is visually evident in the use of marble and intricate carvings. The cost of con-

LOUIS XIV'S LUST FOR WAR

The nature of politics in seventeenth-century Europe fostered wars between most of the major powers as they continued to emerge from the Middle Ages. As countries consolidated their power, redrew their nation's boundaries, and struggled internally with explosive issues of religion and class conflict, warfare became inevitable.

The cost of fighting wars during the seventy-two-year reign of Louis was staggering. Between 1667 and 1713 Louis led France to war against various neighboring states on four occasions. The costs of these wars depleted the national treasury, causing Louis to levy additional taxes on all of the citizenry below the nobility.

There was a side to Louis that many historians interpret as actually enjoying war. Louis invented many victories and denied that some of his defeats ever took place. A tapestry hanging in the Versailles museum depicts Louis victoriously entering the city of Dunkirk on a rearing white horse as Louis points towards columns of French cavalry entering the city, yet what historians find interesting about this tapestry is that Louis did not win Dunkirk in battle; he purchased it from the English in 1662.

In 1676, when Louis led his army in a retreat from the battle of Heurtebise that he feared he would lose, he publicly

struction was carefully recorded by court officials. Robert Berger records the following detailed figures for a single stairway:

> For the marble encrustation of different colors in the walls of the great stairway and of the room above which serves as a landing, with the door-frames and pedestals to carry the captive figures . . . 30,000 *livres.*

> For placing the steps of the said stairway . . . 3,000 *livres.*

> For placing the marble balustrade of which the socle and banister are of white and black marble, and balusters of white and red marble . . . 9,000 *livres.*

> For making a fountain in the niche which is on the landing on the stairway and for placing there a bronze figure . . . 3,000 *livres.*

Although this tapestry shows a victorious Louis entering Dunkirk in battle, he actually purchased the city from the English. Louis often claimed undue victories and denied his military defeats.

stated that the battle was not necessary. Frequently Louis would claim for himself victories his generals had actually won. So obsessed was Louis with warfare that he ordered some of his custom-made shoes with miniature battle scenes painted on the heels.

For pavement of the bottom of the stairway and of the great landing and of the five small ones . . . 22,000 *livres*.

For all the work and ornaments in stucco of the said stairway . . . 25,000 *livres*.

KING'S GUARD ROOM

The King's Guard Room was located between the top of the staircase leading to the king's apartment and the king's bedroom area. Positioned at this strategic location, the guards were able to monitor and control all who wished to be in the presence of the king. In so doing, they positioned themselves well to intercept anyone possibly intending to harm him. Far from having the look of a barracks for housing soldiers, however, the King's Guard Room had an elegance in keeping with the other major rooms of his apartment.

The need to have guards at the ready day and night necessitated the addition of sleeping cots that could be stored out of sight during the day, as well as racks to hold the guards' weaponry. The guards had reason to be on the alert at all times. Not only did the kings of France have their political enemies who might wish to assassinate them, there also were ordinary citizens wandering through the palace from time to time. Although this was the palace of the king, Versailles was open to the public on many occasions.

THE *SALON DE L'OEIL DE BOEUF*

The *Salon de l'Oeil de Boeuf*, the Salon of the Bull's Eye, was so named by Louis XV because of the large oval window at one end of the room. This sixty-five-foot-by-forty-three-foot room served as the anteroom the king, and visitors passed through before entering the king's bedroom. The initial purpose for such a room was to provide a place where nobility awaiting the king's rising ceremony would gather. It later became the room where the gathered nobility commented on the decisions of the king and traded gossip, always watching one another for any sign of how to behave before the king.

This room was originally two rooms that were combined in 1701. The walls are covered with large mirrors and some of the finely carved wood panels. Around the entire room is a six-foot decorative band called a frieze. The decorations of this frieze depict children playing amongst flowers and a geometric waffle-

King Louis XIV's extravagant bedchamber was more than a place to sleep. While still in bed, Louis conducted brief conversations with family members and nobles.

grid. The children are depicted playing musical instruments, playing with dogs, or playfully leaping in the air.

KING'S BEDCHAMBER

Decidedly more than a place to sleep, the king's forty-foot-by-forty-two-foot bedroom was a focal point of Versailles. The king's day began here with a ceremony called the *lever,* or rising, which was a private ritual dictated by rigid etiquette.

Before eight in the morning, when the king awoke, the highest ranking nobles assembled in the *Salon de l'Oeil de Boeuf* to await the king's rising. In this elaborately decorated room, the nobles wandered about in their best formal clothing, exchanging conversation and carefully observing the glances and gestures of the other nobles.

While the nobles nervously awaited the king, one of his attendants would put wood on the fire at about a quarter to eight if there was a chill in the air. Another removed the night candle

The ceremony of lever was conducted each morning. While the king dressed, various officials and nobles approached him. Occasionally the king would receive hundreds of visitors during this morning ritual.

that had burned throughout the night, and a third removed the cot on which his nighttime attendant slept.

At precisely eight, an attendant awoke the king and a small number of close relatives were admitted to the king's bedroom while he was still in his bed. This was their special time to discuss family issues with the king.

At eight fifteen, one of the king's attendants brought in the royal wardrobe for the day, his physician checked the king's health, and the nurse who had cared for him from birth gave him a ceremonial kiss. Following these rituals, the highest-ranking nobles outside the immediate family entered to discuss various topics with the king. After a short religious ceremony, the remainder of the nobles entered for their brief conversations with the king. While still in bed, the king's wig for the day was brought to him. Finally the king got out of bed and sat in a chair where he shaved himself.

At this point, while the king dressed, high-ranking dignitaries such as cardinals, ambassadors, governors, and lesser nobles were allowed to enter. As each approached the king, an attendant whispered the name of the person into the king's ear. While the reception continued, attendants brought in the king's breakfast. While he dressed and ate, as many as two hundred people might have been in the room at any one time.

When he was fully dressed, the king dipped his fingers in holy water and crossed himself, said a prayer, and exited his bedchamber. The *lever* was over. As tedious as this daily ritual could be for those at court, a similar ritual called the *coucher* occurred every night when the king went to bed.

THE QUEEN'S APARTMENT

The role of the queen of France demanded that she have a beautiful and spacious apartment second only to that of the king. The queen's primary responsibility was to take charge of the elaborate social calendar at Versailles. Because the thousands of nobility residing there could not come and go with complete freedom, the king and queen were obligated to provide for their entertainment. This responsibility required the queen to oversee preparations for dinner parties for hundreds within the palace, to plan outdoor festivities for thousands, to entertain visiting kings and queens, to arrange late-night gambling parties, which were the favorites of the royalty, and to organize the entertainment and activities of the children living in the palace. To execute all of these public responsibilities, as well as the private responsibilities of her family, the queen needed a large apartment to take care of all of her needs.

The queen's apartment on the second floor of the palace consisted of four large individual rooms with windows overlooking a southern view of the ornamental gardens. The apartment is reached by way of the Queen's Staircase, which is ornately decorated with different types and colors of marble. All of the

COURT ETIQUETTE

The thousands of nobles residing at Versailles required rules to govern their social behavior, to preserve order, and to prevent chaos from destroying the palace along with their entire class. Etiquette provided this necessary order. Etiquette defined the thousands of silent rules which, although rarely spoken and never written down, were nonetheless learned by everyone from observing the behavior of others. Failure to pay attention to etiquette brought swift punishment upon the offender.

Rules of etiquette dictated virtually all of the behavior and activities of the residents at the palace. The one rule of etiquette overriding all others was the higher the rank of a noble person, the more rights and privileges they were afforded. No other single distinction had greater influence on a person's life at Versailles than their social position, or "orbit," as members of the court often called it.

The orbit of a person, much like that of a planet, was usually constant, rarely moving closer or further away from the king. The orbit determined all of the large issues at Versailles, such as who received the best apartments, who could influence the king's policies, and even whether two young people would be permitted to marry.

This same orbit also controlled all of the frivolous decisions at Versailles. Most notable were seating arrangements for dinner, who walked with whom while strolling in the gardens, and where people stood in various lines for state dinners. When entering a state dinner, either one or both of the double doors of the main salon were opened, depending upon the person's rank. Seating a noble who normally sat close to the king farther away was a sign of punishment for some social infraction.

No one, not even the king, was immune to etiquette. The woman whom Louis XV loved more than any other, Madame de Pompadour, died in 1764. Because she was not the king's wife, she was not afforded a dignified funeral. Louis himself was not allowed publicly to express his sadness. Forbidden by etiquette to attend the funeral, he stood on the balcony in the pouring rain as her cortege returned to Paris. Returning to his room in tears, Louis's attendant heard him say, "That moment was all I am allowed to grieve for her."

queens of France used this staircase, from Marie-Thérèse (1682–1683) to Marie-Antoinette (1770–1789). To care for her apartment and to carry out all of her demands, the queen's staff under Marie-Thérèse totaled 572 servants.

ROOM OF THE QUEEN'S GUARD

The purpose of the Queen's Guard Room, like that of the King's Guard Room, was to provide the living quarters for the soldiers charged with the responsibility of protecting the queen. Within this large room, thirty-seven feet by fifty-four feet, the queen's guard kept watch night and day. Like the King's Guard Room, this elaborately decorated chamber housed the sleeping cots of the guards as well as racks containing their weapons and equipment. The location of this room, at the entrance to the queen's apartment, was conceived to prevent unwanted persons from entering the queen's apartment.

The fact that this room was used for guards did not mean that it lacked the extraordinary decorations found throughout the rest of the palace. The floors of the guards' room were wood parquet with walls covered in either multicolored marble or silk-embroidered cloth. Famed artist Noël Coypel painted the eight panels of the ceiling with scenes taken from Greek and Roman history and mythology.

The most well known incident involving this room occurred when the guards fought heroically to protect their queen in 1789, just before the outbreak of the French Revolution. At that time, an angry mob broke into the palace and tried to force their way into the queen's room. Her guards blocked their entrance and fought the mob in a bloody skirmish, allowing the queen to escape through a back door to safety.

THE *GRAND COUVERT* ANTECHAMBER

The *Grand Couvert* antechamber, measuring forty-nine feet by forty-three feet, was used by the queens of France as the their official reception room to meet the wives of nobility recently admitted to the court at Versailles and to greet visiting nobility. Beginning with Louis XIV, this room served the secondary function of the *Grand Couvert* or public dining room for the king and queen.

In the *Grand Couvert*, the king and queen sat at a table set for two near the large fireplace and ate their dinner, while selected guests from the nobility would watch them eat. Watching the king

The ornate Queen's Guard Room is positioned near the entrance to the queen's apartment. From here, the guards prevented any unwanted persons from entering the royal chamber.

and queen eat was considered an honor by the nobility, and being selected to attend this ceremony was a sign that they were in favor with the king. Some of the nobility attending the *Grand Couvert* recorded their experiences and described the etiquette. Some guests attending this ritual reported that Queen Marie-Antoinette wore white gloves while eating dinner and that she refused to use her napkin, preferring various articles of clothing.

The interior of this room, richly decorated with red fabric covering the walls, contained numerous large paintings and mirrors. The floor was wood parquet and the ceiling was covered by several more paintings. The four corners of the ceiling were rendered in carved wood depictions of war trophies. To illuminate the room, large chandeliers hung from the ceiling.

THE QUEEN'S BEDCHAMBER

The Queen's Bedchamber, roughly a square room forty-three feet on all sides, was primarily used as the place where the queen slept but also witnessed the birth of nineteen royal children. The people of France were aware that their kings fathered many illegitimate children. To be certain that the nobility of France would recognize the queen's children as being legitimate heirs to the throne, the nobles were invited to witness the births of these royal children.

The first childbirth for the queen Marie-Antoinette was attended by so many people that, when the official announcement that the queen was about to give birth was made, the sudden surge of curious spectators nearly overran the bed, causing the royal surgeon to panic.

Of all of the rooms that made up the queen's apartment, this was the most elaborately decorated. The size of this room utterly dwarfed the queen's bed that was set against one of the walls. Designers set a decorative ledge, cantilevered out over the bed, from which hung heavy drapes that could be pulled around the bed during the winter to reduce drafty, cold air.

The south wall had large windows, giving the queen an exquisite view of the sculptured gardens below. The wall decorations were elaborate, with floral designs decorated in gold leaf and large mirrors reflecting the opulence of the room. There was more gold leaf in these ceilings than in any part of the palace's other rooms. Elaborate scenes depicting cherubs interspersed with floral and geometric designs also filled the ceiling.

Widely recognized as the most intricately decorated of all the private apartments, the queen's bedchamber was still no match for the scale and grandeur of the public rooms that Louis built for Versailles. These rooms, built for large gatherings, were the showpieces of the palace, opened to visiting dignitaries and foreign royalty for social events. For these reasons, Louis was willing to spend lavishly to impress all who would experience them.

Public Rooms
of Louis XIV

Psychologists believe that a home is a reliable reflection of the owner's personality. If they are correct, the public rooms of Versailles speak volumes about Louis, who perceived himself to be a king of supreme elegance ruling the world's greatest nation with style and grace. His public rooms—excessively indulgent, elaborately designed, and richly decorated—were precisely an architectural mirror held before the man who built them.

Specifically designed to impress and intimidate, the effectiveness of the entire Versailles experience is demonstrated by the reception of the Russian ambassadors in 1685, recorded by the Marquis de Sourches:

> The Ambassadors of the Grand Duke [Tsar] of Moscow held an audience with the King, in the usual manner, which is to say they came from Paris in the king's carriages, led by the Introducer of the Ambassadors. When they arrived in the front court, two regiments of the guard were there with their arms, and drums sounded when their carriage passed. . . .

> At noon, the Grand Master of Ceremony, with his lieutenants, fetched them and led them up the marble staircase, at the foot of which the captain of the guard received them and led them to the king. The Swiss Guard lined the staircase and they were also in rows in the first two rooms of the apartment of the king, all at arms. The king was in the last room of the apartment seated on a silver chair, set up as a throne, on a platform covered with a magnificent rug of gold, silver, and silk.

> The Muscovites did not approach closer to the king than the foot of the platform, where they prostrated themselves, face down on the floor, in the oriental manner, following which their leader delivered his address. . . .

The Hall of Mirrors has been a favored banquet and reception room from the time of Louis XIV to the present. The floor-to-ceiling stacks of mirrors that line the hall's east side are its distinguishing characteristic.

They were later led back to the room of the Ambassadors, where the king's officers entertained them magnificently; and, after dinner, they were led back to Paris in the same carriages. . . .

Among Louis's favorite public rooms that have survived are the Hall of Mirrors, the chapel, and the royal stables.

THE HALL OF MIRRORS

Illuminated by the light of a thousand candles reflecting off mirrors that extended from floor to ceiling, the Hall of Mirrors has provided a fabled site for state dinners and gala evening parties from the time of Louis XIV to the present. Designed by the architect Mansart and decorated by the painter Le Brun between 1678 and 1686, the Hall of Mirrors replaced a simple passageway used to join the apartments of the king and queen. Well known within the closed royal society during the reign of Louis

THE ROLE OF THE ARCHITECT

Art historians refer to the dominant architectural style of seventeenth-century France as Baroque. The origin of this term is lost, but great elegance, a sense of flourish, and tremendous energy characterize its style. Baroque buildings have undulating walls with decorative surface elements and classical forms such as columns and peristyles.

The architects of Versailles began their design considerations by defining the functions of the different palace areas. Considerations included the types of rooms, how many there would be, their dimensions, access by stairs and hallways, window placement, and orientation. Following the functional design, the architects produced the first drawings.

These first drawings, called footprint drawings, represented the outline of the foundation of the building and the placement of the walls. Produced to scale, they represented the outer perimeter of the building, the precise sizes of the rooms, all walls, and placement of columns and piers carrying the weight of the roof. Architects and engineers used the footprint drawings to estimate the total size of the building, the amount of material needed, the number of workmen required, and the cost of construction.

Following the approval of the footprint drawings, the architects prepared the detailed drawings. These drawings il-

XIV, this hall became famous to the entire Western world 232 years later when, in 1918, the treaty ending World War I, subsequently named the Treaty of Versailles, was signed in this hall.

It is the east side that gives name to the hall. The entire length of this side is set with alternating marble pilasters and bays of mirrors. Each bay consists of a rectangular setting of fifteen mirrors; three mirrors across by five mirrors high. Set on top of this rectangle is a radius of three more mirrors. Mansart's decision to surface the eastern wall with mirrors was not motivated by the wonderful effect he thought they would give to the large room, nor did he include them to create a worldwide reputation.

The idea for a grand hallway was well received by Louis XIV, but with the condition that the focus of the interior be the paintings on the ceiling. For Mansart, the architect behind this and other major architectural features at Versailles, the problem of illuminating a high ceiling raised formidable problems.

lustrated exterior views, details of the outside of the building, and changes in elevation. They also showed the details of the walls, the columns, the windows, the entry doors, and the roofline.

Cross-section drawings illustrated how the building would look if it were cut in half and laid open. These drawings were especially important because they showed the thickness of the walls, the staircases, the supports hidden from the visitor, and the roof.

Engineering drawings, developed to help ensure the safety of the building, illustrated many aspects of its strength. These drawings described the size and thickness of the walls, the types of iron clamps required to hold stone slabs together, the placement of wood braces for constructing arches and domes, and the depth and width of the foundation trenches supporting the entire weight of the building.

Finally, the architects and designers produced the detailed drawings that specified the precise design and measurements of the building's architectural decorations. These drawings showed the details of such things as the column shafts, capitals, and bases, decorative scrollwork cut in the stone, and ornate sculpted elements used to beautify and to grace the building with character.

Mansart's first decision to bring light to the ceiling was to slightly lower the ceiling to forty feet. This would decrease the distance that light would have to be directed to the painted ceiling. His second decision was to place as many windows as practical in the western wall to bring in as much sunlight as possible. The third decision, and the one of greatest aesthetic significance, conceived of the eastern length of the room lined with mirrors to reflect light up to the ceiling from the western windows. It is these mirrors that gave the hall its name. (A rumor circulated at that time, however, explains the use of the mirrors in a very different way. Supposedly, Mansart was embroiled in a personal rivalry with the painter Le Brun, and to spite him, Mansart designed the hall with mirrors so that his rival would have only the ceiling space to paint, rather than the ceiling and the east wall together.)

The highly ornate ceiling, painted by Le Brun forty feet above the wood parquet floor, began with two mythological representations: the labors of Hercules, and Apollo and Diana (the sun and the moon). After considerable work on these two huge panels, Louis decided that they were not appropriate as the primary focus of the room. He ordered Le Brun to redirect his artistic genius toward depicting Louis's own military victories as king of France. Upon hearing the king's order, Le Brun shut himself away for two days before beginning the new ceiling paintings.

The central image of the ceiling depicts Louis wearing Roman armor and seated on a grand throne. Surrounding Louis are women and babies, said to represent the high points of the cultural arts during his reign. To the sides of Louis are storm clouds where three prominent female figures are said to represent European enemies of France. Other panels continue the theme of military triumph during the Dutch War: the crossing of the Rhine, the capture of the city of Maastricht, and the siege of the city of Ghent.

Of the three, the crossing of the Rhine is the most powerful. In this panel, Le Brun depicted Louis as the Greek god Apollo

The hand-painted ceiling panels in the Hall of Mirrors depict Louis's military victories in mythic proportions. One of the most compelling is the rendering of the crossing of the Rhine, with Louis portrayed as the Greek god Apollo (pictured).

charging across the skies in a chariot. Surrounding this central figure is a horde of deities, represented by angels hovering around Louis, while the enemies of France are trampled under the hooves of the four white horses pulling the chariot. The painted ceiling was so dramatic a presentation, that Louis XV, upon one of his returns to Versailles, lay down on the floor to experience the full impact of the work.

AN UNSURPASSED CLIMAX

Grand in scale, the Hall of Mirrors stretches nearly the entire second story length of the western portico of the original central block. Although narrow in size at only 35 feet, its dramatic 246-foot length has a superb western exposure overlooking the formal gardens immediately beneath it and a view toward the horizon beyond the Grand Canal that appears to the viewer to extend forever into the distance. Sunshine streaming through seventeen arched window bays illuminates the hall during the day, and three balconies provide visitors with a view of the famed gardens below. Between the windows inside the hall stood solid silver tables, and under each window sat a solid silver planter containing an orange tree.

The full length of the floor was covered with two enormous carpets; curtains with Louis XIV's monogram lined the windows. These elaborately embroidered curtains contained 130 pounds of gold thread woven into the design. In the evening, seventeen large silver chandeliers and twenty-six smaller ones, bearing a total of one thousand candles, gave a beautiful glow to the room with the light playing off the row of mirrors.

The fine arts historian, Robert Berger, presents the following eloquent sketch of the dramatic impact of the Hall of Mirrors:

> More than anywhere else in the Château, it is in the Galerie des Glaces [Hall of Mirrors] where the visitor of today can best savor the richness and splendor so admired during the reign of the Sun King by Frenchmen and foreigners alike. From its windows and from those of adjacent salons, one can survey from a height large portions of the magnificent formal park that stretches away in three principal directions. The indoors is closely integrated with the outdoors by the abundance of light, reflections, and views, and even by the motif of the central

"A PALACE FOR DUPES"

Although impressively large and opulently decorated, Versailles has had its critics over the years. Henri de Montherlant, in his work, *Service Inutile* (quoted in Pérouse de Montclos's *Versailles*), had this comment to make about the palace:

> Louis XIV was great, without a doubt. But his palace gives no indication of this. It appears to be the work of a social climber advised by a pedant [a pretentious but unimaginative person]—the palace of a middle-class gentleman. Versailles is luxurious, perhaps even majestic, but not great; it could even be said to provide an object lesson in what makes the difference between majesty and grandeur. True grandeur requires a certain pomp, and a certain severity as well. There is pomp at Versailles, but no severity—not even seriousness. Versailles is a palace for the frivolous, a palace for dupes: for those full of their own importance and wealth, but who see no further than their noses. In this overwrought Versailles, an exercise in rhetorical flourish if ever there was one, mediation is not welcome. It appears to the senses and human vanity, nothing more; nothing moves the soul.

painting of Apollo in his quadriga [four horse chariot], an echo of the Apollo Fountain on axis in the Petit Parc [Small Park] and visible from the windows. . . .

Louis XIV walked almost daily in the Galerie des Glaces [Hall of Mirrors]; from this cockpit he could survey the painted history of his reign in the vault [ceiling], the magnificence of French marbles and glass, and the unending expanse of the gardens. The long gallery—a type of room associated with political power—here reaches its unsurpassed climax.

The Hall of Mirrors was the masterpiece of the central block of rooms of the palace, but the north wing of the palace needed a masterpiece as well, and Louis determined that the chapel would serve this purpose.

THE CHAPEL

Third in a long line of chapels at Versailles, Louis XIV's architect, Mansart, began the chapel visitors see today in 1682 and completed it twenty-eight years later in 1710. Second only to the Hall of Mirrors in fame, the chapel is the more striking and stands as the more dominant of the two architectural landmarks at Versailles. Towering above all other rooflines, the chapel is the most notable element of the north wing of the palace, with its peaked roof resembling the keel of an overturned boat.

At that time, religion in Europe was a major focal point of people's spiritual and intellectual energy. All of Europe had followed the teachings of the Catholic Church until the German Martin Luther (1483–1546) challenged several of the basic doctrines of the church. This challenge, often called "The Great Schism" by historians, split the followers of Catholicism into two opposing camps; Catholics who remained obedient to the teachings of Catholicism, and Christians who protested against Catholic interference between themselves and God, and thus came to be called Protestants.

Toward the end of Luther's life, many countries and millions of people broke away from the Catholic Church and established Protestant churches based on Luther's teachings. In France, a predominantly Catholic country, Protestantism gained a small foothold during the latter part of the fifteenth and the beginning of the sixteenth centuries. Those embracing this new religion were called Huguenots and were severely persecuted by the Catholics.

As the religious conflicts continued throughout France, King Henri IV, grandfather of Louis XIV, in an attempt to quell the warfare, issued the Edict of Nantes in 1598, granting some freedoms to the Huguenots. The edict granted them the right to build churches in certain cities, to hold services in their homes, to hold political positions in local governments, and to build four universities. In addition, one hundred fortified cities were given to them as a gesture of security.

For a short period of time the edict quieted the conflict, but in 1689, Louis XIV revoked the Edict of Nantes, once again inflaming the feud between the Catholics and Huguenots. Finally, most of the Huguenots fled France for the safety of Protestant countries, including the colonies in America.

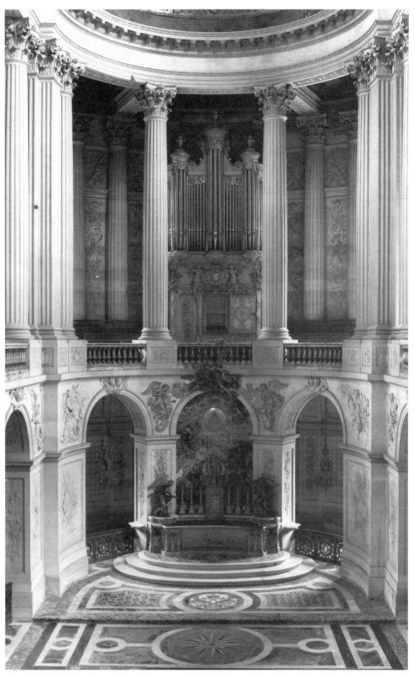

Louis built the chapel on the grounds of Versailles to show his commitment to the Catholic Church. This photo shows the chapel's marble floor and square piers topped by Corinthian columns.

Amidst all of this turmoil, Louis resolved to build a chapel at Versailles that would make a definitive statement about his commitment to the Catholic Church. Not content to build a chapel merely for worship, he resolved to build an imposing statement to the supremacy of Catholicism in France. In relation to the scale of the palace, the chapel suggests an enormous cavern.

The floor, decorated in a geometric design of polychrome marble dominated by deep green accents, is the most impressive in the palace. Looking up to the ceiling, worshippers and visitors see an elaborately painted set of panels depicting allegorical figures from classical literature. With cherubs and angels swirling in colorful scenes depicting highlights of French history and culture, these paintings are consistent with the style of ceiling paintings found in the Hall of Mirrors. The enormous weight of the roof is supported on the ground floor by massive, white square piers, above which Corinthian columns bear the weight of the architrave.

The need for light in a chapel this size was a concern to the architect, Mansart. To flood the chapel with light during the day, he designed large windows along both sides of the chapel on all three levels. Unlike many chapels in Paris of that time, famous for their colorful stained glass, the glass in the Versailles chapel is clear to maximize the admission of light.

As the palace took shape, defined by remarkably imaginative rooms such as the Hall of Mirrors and the chapel, Louis began looking for new building projects. He steadfastly believed that all new projects should express the same high standards set by the craftsmen who built the palace, even building projects for the stabling of his royal horses.

THE STABLES

Erected by the architect Mansart between 1679 and 1682, the two royal stables accommodated the king's prized horses, bred for hunting, warfare, and pulling his elaborately bejeweled carriages. These two stables, the Great Stables for housing the king's riding horses and the Small Stables for housing his carriages and carriage horses, are massive in scale. They are so unexpectedly large that first-time visitors approaching the palace along the three avenues converging at the grand entry often mistook them for the palace itself. Far more than mere stables, these were monuments to the king's most prized possessions, his horses.

The king's horses were symbols of both personal and national pride. Used variously for hunting, transportation, warfare, festive parades, and casual riding, they were bred for size, speed, and beauty. All of the kings of France spent lavishly on the breeding, training, and care of their mounts. Horses not only had the practical value of providing transportation for hunting and warfare, but the additional value of social status. The more horses a person owned, and the better the quality of the horses, the greater the prestige of the owner. No one had a better stable of horses nor more social prestige than did the king.

Mansart designed these two stables on a colossal scale to accommodate a large number of horses and to impress the king's visitors. The modern French historian Guy Walton states that they were capable of housing about twelve thousand horses. This extremely high estimate conflicts with that of the historian Jean-Marie Pérouse de Montclos, who estimates that the two stables held seven hundred horses during the reign of Louis XIV and two thousand under his grandson Louis XVI.

PORTRAIT OF LOUIS XIV

Court historian and gossip, Saint-Simon, gave insight into the personality of Louis XIV from time to time in his *Mémoires*. In this excerpt, Saint-Simon eulogizes Louis's athletic abilities,

> He was very fond of fresh air and exercise, as much as he could take. He excelled at dancing and at badminton, as well as tennis. Old as he was, he still rode well. He liked to see all of these activities executed with grace and style. He was fond of archery and no one could handle a bow and arrow with greater mastery and grace. He was especially partial to hunting stags, which he pursued in an open carriage after having broken his arm while pursuing one on foot at the Fontainebleau palace after the death of the queen. When hunting from the carriage, he did so alone, commanding the four horses by himself at a dead run, and he did so with a skill and deftness exceeding the best coachmen, and was marked by his usual grace.

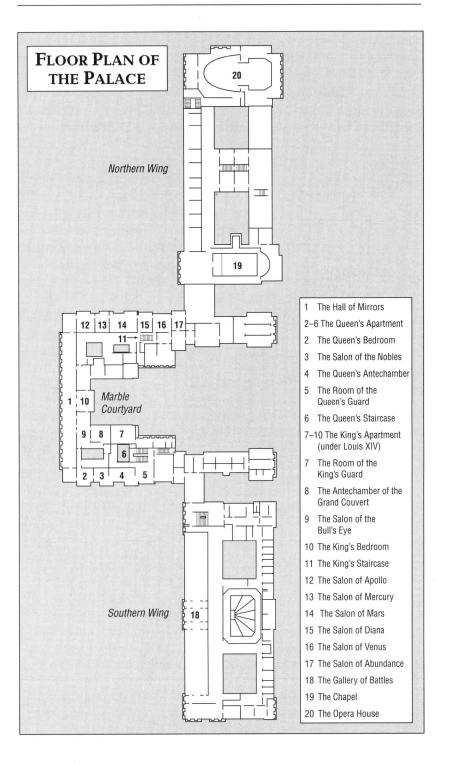

FLOOR PLAN OF THE PALACE

Northern Wing

20

19

Marble Courtyard

12 13 14 15 16 17
11→

1 10

9 8 7
6
2 3 4 5

Southern Wing   18

1   The Hall of Mirrors

2–6 The Queen's Apartment

2   The Queen's Bedroom

3   The Salon of the Nobles

4   The Queen's Antechamber

5   The Room of the
    Queen's Guard

6   The Queen's Staircase

7–10 The King's Apartment
    (under Louis XIV)

7   The Room of the
    King's Guard

8   The Antechamber of the
    Grand Couvert

9   The Salon of the
    Bull's Eye

10 The King's Bedroom

11 The King's Staircase

12 The Salon of Apollo

13 The Salon of Mercury

14 The Salon of Mars

15 The Salon of Diana

16 The Salon of Venus

17 The Salon of Abundance

18 The Gallery of Battles

19 The Chapel

20 The Opera House

Pérouse de Montclos also explains that the horses boarded here belonged exclusively to the king, there being separate stables for those of the queen and princes.

To administer to all of the needs of the horses, Louis XIV maintained a large and complex staff of stable hands under the direction of a stable master who was called Monsieur le Grand. Directly under him were the hundreds of stable hands required to attend to the needs of the horses, as well as the ceremony that accompanied the king as he traveled the countryside. Care for the horses at the stables required the skills of veterinarians, blacksmiths, saddle and harness makers, feeders, trainers, and grooms. Accompanying the king on his travels were drummers and trumpeters, armed guards, cloak bearers, and numerous other attendants caring for the needs of the king.

This bronze statue of Jules Hardouin-Mansart depicts the Versailles architect reviewing his plans.

The construction of the stables, considered by many architects to have been Mansart's masterpiece, was as beautiful and elaborate as the palace itself. The royal horses entered their stables by way of the huge horseshoe-shaped cobblestone courtyard. Once in the courtyard, they entered the stables through dozens of arched entries built of stone blocks. Above each entry, Mansart set windows and above those were dormers on the roof to provide additional light. The interiors of the stables were built of solid stone with arches and barrel vaults running the entire length of the main hallways. Mansart designed the hallways to be wide enough to accommodate four horses side by side. They are about twenty feet wide and rise to a height of thirty feet.

Within the stables, ornate decorations duplicating Greek and Roman columns and other architectural features impressed royal guests. Wooden stalls covered with richly tooled leather inscribed with the names of the horses provided luxurious housing for the royal chargers. Numerous fireplaces were scattered through the stables to heat the stalls during the winter.

LOUIS XIV'S PLACE IN FRENCH HISTORY

How was Louis able to commit so much money over so many years to build a palace paid for by the poor but that only the very rich enjoyed? Why did no one, nor any group of advisors, oppose the building of Versailles on the grounds that the cost for such an extravagant building program might have been better spent on projects of benefit to all French citizens? Historians find the answer to these questions in both the immediacy of Louis's personality and in regal custom as far back as the fifteenth century when kings increasingly exerted royal authority over the nobility.

As the kings of Europe further consolidated their authority, the aristocracy determined that the king's sole opinion in making all laws and for governing the country was preferable to many conflicting opinions. Gradually, two doctrines of leadership emerged that bestowed upon the king the authority to act unilaterally and without fear of contradiction; absolutism and the divine right of kings.

ABSOLUTISM AND THE DIVINE RIGHT OF KINGS

Absolutism is the political doctrine that endows total authority into the hands of a single ruler. Under such a system, all citizens obey the king's authority absolutely. This does not mean that Louis did not consult with his advisors—he often did—but once he made a decision, no advisor had the authority to challenge or reverse it. In this sense, absolutism is the opposite of democracy, which places political control into the hands of the citizens and their elected representatives. An absolute ruler like Louis XIV did not have a

Because he was absolute ruler of France, Louis could spend as much of the nation's wealth on his dreams for Versailles as he wished. No governing body in France could challenge his authority.

Supreme Court or Congress to prevent him from acting unreasonably. No individual or group of individuals was able to constrain Louis in any way. His absolute rule, coupled with his control over both the treasury and the bureaucracy that carried out his political directives, elevated France to a position of power and stability greater than all other European rivals.

Several philosophers supported absolutism, the most widely read being the English philosopher Thomas Hobbes (1588–1679), who became interested in the struggle between kings and their subjects. He wrote that the only way for a country to avoid wars, riots, and other forms of chaos was to allow the king to rule with absolute authority and that the people must submit to the king's absolute supremacy in all matters. Without a king, wrote Hobbes, humankind

> is in that condition called war, and such a war is man against man. In such condition . . . there is no knowledge of the earth, no account of time, no arts, no literature, no society, and what is worst of all, continual fear, danger of violent death, and the life of man is solitary, poor, nasty, brutish, and short.

Louis XIV's declaration *L'état, c'est moi*, "I am the state," summarized his perception of absolute rule.

The doctrine of the divine right of kings expresses the belief system that God selects kings as his representatives and that they derive their right to rule from God. According to this doctrine, a king is neither subject to the control of his advisors nor the will of his subjects; he is responsible to God alone. Indirectly, it states the view that the king's authority is the only force that makes society function as God had intended.

The doctrine of divine right of kings, coupled with the doctrine of absolutism, armed Louis with unabridged authority to indulge his passion for building at Versailles. No advisor, not even the queen herself, dared to mount serious opposition to the amount of money Louis spent on Versailles. Louis's passion for building went beyond the Palace of Versailles to encompass the expansive gardens surrounding the palace.

As visitors approached the estate in their richly decorated horse-drawn carriages, they could see the magnitude of the palace in the distance, stretching more than a quarter of a mile from north to south wings. What they could not see on their approach, nor could they possibly imagine, were the nineteen thousand acres of gardens east of the palace, which many believed were a far more awe-inspiring work of art than the palace itself.

THE GARDENS

In its heyday, the Palace of Versailles was the central attraction of this grand estate during the evenings, but during the days the central attraction was the gardens. The apartments in the palace for everyone except the royal family and close relatives were small. In the summer, the occupants sweltered in the heat of their rooms and in the winter, they lacked adequate heat. Some of the apartments lacked both fireplaces and windows, creating unhealthy conditions that led to illness and, in some cases, death. For escape, the noble families needed out-of-door activities during the day, such as exercise, socializing, parties, theater productions, and hunting.

The nobility preferred to spend as much of their daylight time as possible in the vast stretches of open space encompassing the magnificently designed parks, formal gardens, and hunting grounds. This expansive network of gardens, embellished by fountains, statues, and footpaths, created an enchanting atmosphere that many found far more pleasurable than the palace itself.

Louis XIV had foreseen the need for these elegant gardens surrounding the château. He knew they would play an important role occupying the time of the nobility living there. He also saw these open spaces as an elaborate backdrop for showing off the grandeur, wealth, and power of the king of France to visiting kings and queens. With these two objectives in mind, he hired the world's foremost landscape architects to convert his immense estate into the world's most extravagant garden. Louis hired the architect André Le Nôtre (1613–1700) to oversee the design of the gardens. Le Nôtre designed them to represent to all visitors the high cultural standards of the most powerful nation in Europe and to represent the most powerful king. Foreign leaders visiting Versailles went home telling stories of Louis XIV's endless wealth and absolute authority.

Before any work began, Le Nôtre and his staff spent months riding the entire estate with Louis to be certain that he fully

The elaborate gardens of Versailles took months to map out and design. Architect André Le Nôtre planned the gardens as a place for the nobles to socialize.

understood the wishes of the king. He then spent months drawing the site, adding all of the architectural features Louis wished to have. He took this approach to ensure that everything the king wanted would be included and to ensure that everything would be in proper scale and harmony.

Drawing the entire estate accurately was challenging because the acreage was so vast that no one could find an elevation high enough to see all of it at one time. The French historian, Jean-Marie Pérouse de Montclos writes, "When Louis XIV first expressed interest in Versailles, it consisted of 2,471 acres. Upon his death, the formal gardens covered 235 acres, the 15 small parks were 4,200 acres, and the hunting park, 14,827 acres."

To solve the problem of drawing the 19,262-acre estate, his assistants drew a series of smaller maps, each representing one parcel of the property. When they had completed them all, they combined them into a single map representing the entire acreage. Le Nôtre then took the map and directed artists to redraw it, adding a bird's-eye view so that he and his assistants would have a more accurate perspective showing the changing elevations. Artists then completed both the final versions of the small maps and the final large map using watercolors. The famed twentieth-century novelist, poet, and filmmaker Jean Cocteau, composer of the text for the light and sound spectacle presented at Versailles during summer evenings in the 1960s,

PUBLIC ACCESS TO VERSAILLES

Although the kings lived far from the common people, they nonetheless believed that the king's residence and gardens belonged to the whole nation. Jean-Marie Pérouse de Montclos quotes the English historian and traveler Arthur Young, who had this to say about seeing commoners at Versailles in his book, *Travels in France During the Years 1787, 1788, 1789*:

> It was amusing to see the blackguard figures that were walking uncontrolled about the palace, and even his bed chamber; men whose rags betrayed them to be in the last stage of poverty, and I was the only person that stared and wondered how the devil they got there.

This open access to the palace created serious security and health risks. To control the royal apartments used by the king and queen, bodyguards were posted in guardrooms at the top of the staircase leading to their rooms. While the king and queen walked the gardens, their bodyguards accompanied them to keep unwanted visitors from intruding. In addition to occasional threats to the lives of royalty, theft became an increasing problem at Versailles. Most commonly, stolen items were small, such as plumbing fixtures that looters could take easily. Besides theft, there occurred vandalism to statues, fountains, and other art forms scattered about the gardens.

Public access to areas of the main palace and gardens taxed the limited sanitation resources. Bathrooms with running water were in limited supply, leaving most people to use chamber pots later emptied by palace servants. In a 1764 book titled *The Policing of Beggars*, La Morandiere, here quoted by Christopher Hibbert, informs that, "One is revolted by the disgusting odors hanging over the park, the garden, and even the château itself. Passageways, corridors, and hallways are full of urine and fecal matter . . . the lowest dregs of the population relieve themselves before other people without shame or restraint."

wrote of Le Nôtre, "There was a swamp. And there were architects and gardeners. And there were lines, angles, triangles, rec-
tangles, circles, and pyramids. And there was a park, and this
park was born of the soul of Le Nôtre."

After Le Nôtre had completed all of the design work, he created a general layout for the gardens along two axes: a main
axis running east/west and a secondary one running north/south.
He then proposed to complete the job in three phases: closest to
the palace would be the formal gardens called *parterres*, a short
distance from the palace, the small parks called *bousquets*, and
farthest from the palace, the hunting park.

FORMAL GARDENS

Closest to the palace, the formal gardens were the centerpiece for
the entire estate. Le Nôtre designed these gardens to be viewed
by the king and his court from their nearby apartments and to provide open spaces where people could enjoy walking while they
viewed the palace and socialized with their friends. To accomplish

*The centerpiece of Louis's huge estate, the 235 acres of formal gardens were divided into
five terraces. The Water Terrace can be seen centered in front of the palace, while the Latona Terrace appears at the bottom of the photo.*

CLEARING THE SWAMP

Long before crews planted the first trees, they leveled large parcels of land, tore out existing trees and shrubs, and drained swampy areas. As many as thirty-six thousand workers, assisted by six thousand horses toiling full time worked for years to move millions of cubic yards of earth and mud. The workers were primarily peasants from throughout France who came to Versailles to work on the project. During times when France was at peace, soldiers joined the peasants hauling dirt, digging trenches, and building structures to carry and store the huge quantities of water required for the project.

Hauling mud and dirt all day long, month after month, year after year, took its toll. Many workers died from diseases found in the mud. Mosquitoes carrying other deadly diseases were a constant threat. Falls killed some and others, trapped waste deep in thick muck, were crushed when they could not move quickly enough out of the way of horses and carts. The contemporary historian Pierre-André Lablaude adds, "With thousands of horses plowing the earth and tearing up unwanted brush, it was said that some were actually buried alive in the mud and mounding of earth." Others were buried alive under massive mudslides.

The French historian Jean-Marie Pérouse de Montclos reports that the cost in terms of lives lost was high. The official recorded number of deaths over one twenty-year period was 227. Each surviving family received between forty and one hundred *livres* as compensation for each dead worker. One peasant mother who lost a son criticized the king because the compensation for his death was so small. The king, upon hearing her criticism, ordered that she be publicly whipped. Other protesters had their tongues cut out. Pérouse de Montclos goes on to cite Madame Sévigné, who wrote in her diary about the terrible conditions: "There was a high death rate of the construction workers whose bodies are carried away every night by the wagonloads. This is concealed as much as possible in order not to alarm the other workmen."

THE ORANGERIE—LOUIS XIV'S OBSESSION WITH ORANGES

Orange trees requiring a warm climate were a favorite of the king, who ordered his architect, Mansart, to build them a heated enclosure for the winter. This building, called the Orangerie, was 510 feet long and 69 feet wide; large enough to protect the two thousand orange trees from the winter cold. In keeping with all of the structures that Mansart designed at Versailles, the Orangerie expressed an exquisitely ornate design befitting the most ornate palatial estate in Europe.

Like Versailles itself, the Orangerie represents a huge extravagance. Unable to survive the winter climate, the orange trees had to be moved inside every winter.

Planted in large wooden boxes and stored in the Orangerie during the winter, workmen wheeled out the king's favorites at the beginning of spring when the fragrance from the blooming orange trees was especially strong. In the spring and summer, gardeners moved them out of doors, placing them in areas close to the palace where walkers could enjoy their fragrance. Along favorite pathways, the orange trees were placed in rows alternating each tree with a marble urn. He even ordered them placed inside the Hall of Mirrors.

So enamored was Louis with his trees that when he once heard that another man owned an orange tree larger than any of his own, he ordered the tree brought to him. In early winter, the orange trees returned to the Orangerie where they would again be safe from the winter frost. Louis later extended this sort of climate control to his seven hundred fig trees as well.

both of these objectives, he placed these gardens on flat terraces or *parterres* so residents and visitors could view them without obstructions. Le Nôtre divided the 235 acres into five large terraces, later named the Water Terrace, the North Terrace, the South Terrace, Latona's Terrace, and the Orangerie Terrace.

After workers had leveled the five terraces, they installed miles of underground pipes to carry water to the many fountains. Archaeologists working at Versailles have uncovered three types of pipe: brass, iron, and wood. The oldest and least reliable were the wood pipes. Workers could not successfully join them together to prevent leaks and they rotted quite quickly underground. The brass and iron pipes lasted much longer and workers were able to join each of them with water-tight seals. So many miles of pipe were needed that factories sprang up to supply them exclusively for Versailles. Workers dug several large reservoirs to capture and store water that was released through the system of pipes when the pools needed filling or when the fountains were activated.

GEOMETRIC DESIGNS

The formal gardens were within view of the palace and, for this reason, Le Nôtre meticulously designed them to be orderly, well manicured, and color-ful. The order he employed was that of geometry. All paths were either parallel or intersecting at precise right angles. All round pools were precise circles. Many of the designs for paths, plants, and pools were symmetrical to present mirror images. All shrubs were planted in straight lines and none grew more than two feet high. Gardeners shaped them to look like inverted ice-cream cones, planted them in even numbers, and spaced them evenly.

The formal gardens of Versailles were meticulously manicured. These shrubs, kept exactly as they would have been in Louis's day, are in straight, even rows and are in precise cone shapes.

Each terrace had a unique design that could be best viewed from the second floor of the palace. At the center of each terrace was a pool with jets of water to cool the hot summer air. Around each pool, low hedges no more than one foot high swirled and looped to create intricate floral designs that were outlined by colorful flowering plants. Punctuating these hedges and flowers were short evergreen shrubs sculpted into precise cone shapes. Low marble walls separated the planted areas from the walk-ways. The walkways of crushed, colored gravel directed the flow of visitors throughout the sculpted gardens. At each corner of the terrace, Le Nôtre placed a large sculpted stone vase.

To maintain this perfect geometry and manicured appearance, Le Nôtre employed a staff of hundreds of gardeners to daily swarm over these gardens before they filled with residents out for their morning walks. The gardeners would inspect each shrub, plant, and tree for leaves or flowers that appeared to be out of place. When gardeners had completed the clipping, a cleanup crew picked up the leaves, raked the paths, and turned on the water jets. If the king wished to awake one morning to see all yellow flowers in the formal gardens instead of all red ones, a crew would have to work all night to replant them.

SMALL PARKS

In contrast to the formal, well-manicured geometric layout of the formal gardens, Le Nôtre saw a need for slightly more casual gardens. He created fifteen small parks or *bousquets* as secluded, heavily wooded areas with trees rising fifty to one hundred feet tall. He created them as mini theme parks for the enjoyment of the residents and visitors at Versailles. The themes he borrowed were taken from the French, Greek, Roman, and Egyptian cultures. Each park was several hundred acres, large enough for many people to walk, ride their horses, or to enjoy them from carriages. These parks surrounded the formal gardens and totaled more than four thousand acres.

Le Nôtre intended the entry into each of the parks to be an adventure for the visitors. Surrounded by high mature trees, Louis XIV wanted it to be an experience for visitors akin to entering a giant maze filled with surprises at every turn. Louis took such delight in this that he closely supervised the design of each park. The paths meandering through the parks frequently made sharp turns or wound around water fountains, statuaries, grottos, and entertainment areas before arriving at the interior of the park.

Le Nôtre described his many masterpieces of landscape architecture, known for their groves of trees mingled with canals of water, in his notebook: "They [the canals] snake around freely and twist around trees in wide open spaces, with fountains here and there, . . . a cool place ladies go to work, play, and have something to eat . . . it is the only garden I know of where it is nice to walk, as well as being the loveliest."

Finding enough trees to plant was as difficult a task as finding enough workers to move and plant them. Royal gardeners

GARDEN PARTIES

When Louis XIV was a young king, his favorite use for the royal gardens was as a setting for parties. To create a festive atmosphere, Louis decorated the formal gardens close to the palace with fountains and statuaries. At first the statues were of limestone, but in time he replaced them with statues of more expensive materials such as bronze and marble.

Louis loved elaborate productions and loved to show off his new palace to all of France. The best musicians, cooks, decorators, and performers were summoned to Versailles to stage the parties. Louis insisted that each party be different, larger, and more opulent than the previous one.

In 1664, Louis gave a party lasting nine days. Each day had a different theme and was presented in a different part of the gardens. Stages were erected in the mornings, and at night, when the guests were back inside the palace, were torn down to make way for a new stage the following morning. Thousands of workers scurried about during the night tearing out flowers of one color and replacing them with those of a different color for the next day's events. Three plays written by Molière were produced to the delight of the visitors.

Following the plays, dinner consisting of five courses of fifty-six different dishes, was served to all of the guests. Following the dinner, musicians played while guests danced to music accompanied by the babble of the water fountains. Near the end of the festivities, Louis ordered the lighting of thousands of candles hidden throughout the bushes. As a final signal that the party was ending, a thunderous fireworks display illuminated the night sky, directing the nobility back to their apartments.

uprooted tens of thousands of mature trees throughout France for replanting at Versailles. Louis demanded so many mature trees that some nobles criticized him behind his back for the deplorable theft. Workers uprooted and carted elm, oak, beech, orange, and lemon trees to Versailles for replanting. The transportation was carried out in such a rough manner that the majority died shortly after their arrival. If Louis did not like a particular type of tree, he ordered gardeners to replace it with another species. This brazen violation of France's landscape caused Saint-Simon to comment in his *Mémoires*, "It allowed him [Louis] to ride roughshod over nature and to use his riches and wiliness to subdue nature to his likes. Who would not be disgusted and sickened at this violence against nature?"

Two of Louis's favorite small parks, which required thousands of specialty trees, were the Labyrinth and the Garden of the King. The Labyrinth Park was one of the most popular and unusual of the small parks designed by Le Nôtre. He designed it to be a maze that people could walk thorough. Within the thickly wooded maze he incorporated thirty-nine fountains, to the delight of first-time visitors who followed the pathway as it wound its way through the trees. Each fountain illustrated one of the fables of Aesop in sculpture form. The path began in one corner and led visitors along a 2,468-foot-long mazelike adventure past each fountain without passing the same one twice. Each of the fountains had a tablet on which was inscribed the story of the fable depicted. To complete them on schedule, eighteen sculptors worked on the fountains, carving 333 representations of animals, each painted in its natural color.

At the southern edge of the small parks, Le Nôtre constructed the King's Garden between 1671 and 1683. It contained two large pools hidden deep within a wooded forest of mature oak, beech, and elm, transplanted from other regions of France. A path separated the two pools. From the two pools, Le Nôtre designed eighteen more paths radiating out to the four sides of the park. The central attraction that delighted visitors to this

Louis was especially fond of fountains and pools, placing over fourteen hundred throughout the Versailles complex.

park was the numerous fountains shooting jets of water thirty feet into the air. Visitors enjoying the view would stroll around the pools, with the water jets providing cool breezes on hot summer afternoons. Occasionally, children paddled small boats and chased exotic swans who lived in the pools. Six life-sized statues representing Greek and Roman gods and goddesses decorated the perimeter of the pools.

HUNTING PARK

The hunting park was the largest part of the royal estate and Le Nôtre placed it farthest from the palace. Occupying two-thirds of the entire estate, a twenty-seven-mile-long wall with twenty-two guarded entrances surrounded this 14,827-acre parcel. Originally used as a place where the nobility hunted wild game, it later evolved into a large wooded area for pleasure riding on horseback and in carriages. Unlike the formal gardens close to the palace and the small parks surrounding the formal gardens, the hunting park was not as meticulously designed or maintained.

THE GRAND CANAL

The central focus of the hunting park was the Grand Canal. Its construction took place between 1667 and 1671, and in keeping with the extraordinary scale of the hunting park, the Grand Canal was huge. Built in the form of a cross, the east-west axis was 4,937 feet long by 204 feet wide, with the north-south axis measuring 3,291 feet long by 204 feet wide.

Set directly on a visual line with the royal apartments in the palace, the king and his family could see the Grand Canal in the distance, beyond the small parks and even farther beyond the formal gardens. With a length of nearly one mile on each axis, the canal appeared to extend all the way to the horizon.

The task of digging the canal was one of the most difficult due to the thick reeds and mud that trench diggers had to remove. After the workers had excavated the canal to the desired depth, they set clay tiles on the bottom and sides to contain clean water and to prevent the return of reeds and mud.

The Grand Canal quickly became a favorite place for the nobility to play, especially for their children. A fleet of brightly painted boats of many different types dotted the water. Those favored by the guests were the gondolas, gifts from the government of Venice, Italy, and others modeled after the French warships of the time. Taking boat rides was a favorite pastime and became so popular that Louis had to build dormitories to house the crews that sailed them.

WATERWORKS

The sight of water fountains and geysers captivated Louis XIV. He scattered more than fourteen hundred fountains and pools throughout his thirty square miles of gardens and forests. The three fountains that were his favorites were the Fountains of Apollo, the Fountains of Latona, and the Fountains of Neptune.

These plans show the entire layout of Versailles. The dark cross in the center of the illustration is the Grand Canal, and the stables are shown at the bottom.

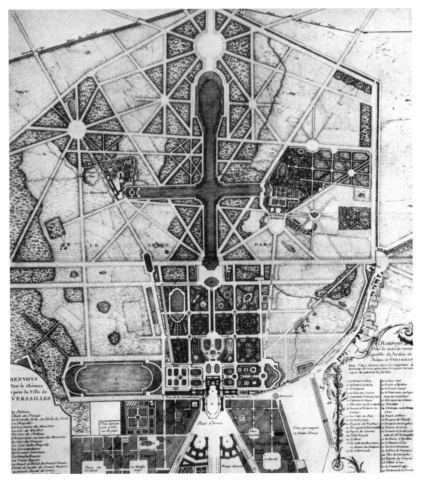

These three occupied a central location on the château's main promenade. Massive in size and of extraordinary complexity, they sprayed a million gallons of water an hour when in use. The Fountains of Neptune had 109 jets spraying water simultaneously. Some fountains were capable of spraying water eighty-five feet into the air.

Few things in life delighted Louis more than inviting kings and queens from rival countries to visit his splendid estate. One of his favorite tours given to visiting royalty included long walks through miles of ornately decorated footpaths. Beginning with the formal gardens close to the palace, they wound their way through several of the small theme parks, along the Grand Canal, through dense forests, along pools of water, and past statuaries depicting Greek and Roman themes. To the delight of the unsuspecting visitors, the highlights of these casual wanderings were always the dozens of fountains cascading water at every turn.

THE MENAGERIE

To the delight of the residents of Versailles and to its visitors, Louis XIV decided in 1663 that the gardens needed a menagerie or zoo. The task of designing the zoo fell to the architect Le Vau, who began by constructing a slate-domed octagon with cages radiating out from each of the eight sides. The first animals to arrive were exotic birds, like ostriches, pelicans, and storks, followed by more exotic animals such as camels and lions, and later in the eighteenth century, rhinoceros and elephants. Getting to the zoo was as much fun for the children living at Versailles as the zoo itself. Visitors boarded gondolas at the eastern end of the Grand Canal near the palace and floated down the canal to the zoo. In addition, the zoo was also used for early scientific investigations of its animals.

As the gardens of Versailles expanded in size and popularity, the nobility passed more of their idle time enjoying the gardens' benefits and the construction of the Grand Canal and the Menagerie. The success of these two new attractions encouraged Louis XIV and his successors to take advantage of available space in the hunting park for further expression of their passion for building. Louis, in keeping with his nature, responded with unrestrained enthusiasm for more palaces, more gardens, and more entertainment in a corner of the hunting park named for a village that had once stood there, Trianon.

THE TRIANON COMPLEX

The Trianon complex, built largely by Louis XIV, is yet another example of compounded magisterial excess. Not satisfied with the largest and most opulent palace in Europe, Louis required more palaces to satisfy his needs for grandeur and privacy. Not satisfied with the most ornate gardens ever designed, Louis required more of them to compliment his newly built palaces. Not satisfied with the simple diversions and parties of his early years, Louis now sought grandiosity that many privately considered inappropriate, even for the king of France.

To find enough real estate for this complex of palaces and gardens exhibiting various shapes and sizes, Louis purchased the town of Trianon in 1668, when he was just thirty years old. This entire town, about a mile and a half from the main palace, became the northwest corner of Louis's Versailles estate. In his haste to begin construction on the first of four royal structures, he evicted the town's people, demolished the town's buildings, and began a whole new building project purely for his personal indulgence. Why would a king who already had one of the greatest palaces at his disposal want to build others?

French historians agree that this question has many answers. Louis's principal palace at Versailles did not provide him with the privacy he needed. Although the primary residence for him and the queen, it was also the residence for the five thousand nobles making up the court who shared the palace and its resources. The nobles, although living there at the command of the king, lived lives that demanded the attention of Louis and his staff. Far more people wanted the attention of the king for both political and social favors than Louis could possibly accommodate. Historians believe that the persistent intrusions of the court into the lives of the royal family provided the primary reason he sought refuge from the very people he required to live close to him.

An ambassador is received at Versailles. Louis built the Trianon complex to escape from having to attend to the needs of such visitors.

THE COURT OF VERSAILLES

The concept of the court at Versailles was unique to this period of European history. The term "court" referred to both the actual physical place where all decisions affecting France were made and to the individuals making the decisions; in this case the king and his key advisors. Their decisions encompassed making and enforcing laws, raising taxes, declaring wars, resolving internal disputes, and generally overseeing the social well-being of the king's subjects, both the peasantry and the nobility. A French royal official in the seventeenth century wrote, "Wherever the king was, there was also his court, and wherever was his court, there also was his council."

France, at that time in its history, did not have a designated capital city as it does today in Paris. Under Louis XIV, the court met at Versailles and modern historians refer to it as the Court of Versailles. Under Louis's predecessors, the court met in many different cities in France, such as Saint-Germain, referred to as the Court of Saint-Germain. This migratory court required the members to meet with the king at one location, return home to attend to personal business, and to reconvene with the court at a different location in France. This transient quality was particularly problematic during prolonged wars ranging over large tracts of territory.

The revolutionary change made by Louis XIV in 1682 was to permanently move the court to Versailles, thereby also forcing all of the nobility to reside there permanently. This significant change forced Louis to provide for all of the court's needs and initiated his seemingly endless building programs. Having once housed his entire court at Versailles, Louis created the problem of controlling them; and once having controlled them, Louis had successfully forced them to trade down their political authority to nothing more than social authority.

THE PORCELAIN TRIANON

Louis intended the first Trianon building, designed by the architect Le Vau, to serve as a one-day escape from the main Versailles palace. The new palace acquired the name Porcelain Trianon because its Chinese-influenced design called for the exterior to be covered in blue and white porcelain tiles. Chinese architecture, although rare in Europe, was not without precedent. France at this time had established trade agreements with China that saw the importation of brightly colored tiles, silk, lacquered furniture, and vases painted with Chinese themes. So popular was the invasion of Chinese art that the local French artisans quickly learned how to imitate their products for consumption by the French aristocracy. Louis became so enamored with Chinese art and architecture that he sometimes enjoyed comparing himself to the great emperors of China.

The design of this small palace suggests its use. There were only two types of rooms: apartments and rooms dedicated to food service. Designed for short stays for a small number of people, the king and queen used the two apartments as private retreats from the crowds at the palace. It is also a well-documented fact that Louis used the apartments as hideaways for illicit affairs with other women. The prominence of the rooms for food service indicates that major activities here were special occasion dinners. The series of smaller rooms designed to store and serve food and drinks suggests the types of foods favored by royalty: They included rotisseries for roasting meats, bakeries designed exclusively for pastries, containers for the cool storage of fruits, and elaborately decorated pots for jams and jellies.

Louis XIV's passion for gardens carried over to the Porcelain Trianon. The historian of the time, Saint-Simon, tells us in his *Mémoires* that Louis insisted that the flowers be changed each day to satisfy his needs for variety. So large was this quantity of fragrant flowers that Saint-Simon remarks that the fragrance could be so strong that visitors sometimes had to flee far from the little palace to find a breath of fresh air. Several historians have reported that, at the height of its use, the number of plants at the Porcelain Trianon numbered well over one million.

THE LARGE TRIANON

In 1687, seventeen years after the completion of the diminutive Porcelain Trianon, Louis XIV ordered his architect Mansart to tear down the Porcelain Trianon and to replace it with a newer

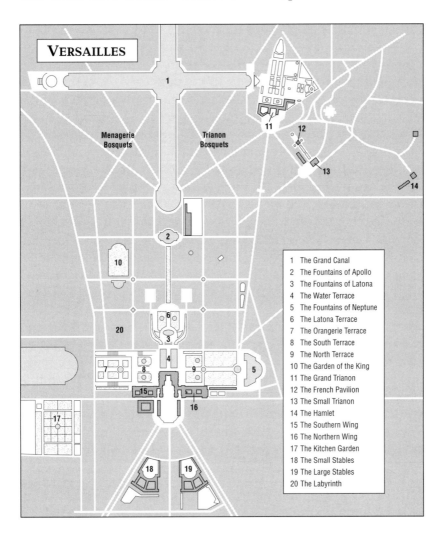

VERSAILLES

Menagerie Bosquets

Trianon Bosquets

1 The Grand Canal
2 The Fountains of Apollo
3 The Fountains of Latona
4 The Water Terrace
5 The Fountains of Neptune
6 The Latona Terrace
7 The Orangerie Terrace
8 The South Terrace
9 The North Terrace
10 The Garden of the King
11 The Grand Trianon
12 The French Pavilion
13 The Small Trianon
14 The Hamlet
15 The Southern Wing
16 The Northern Wing
17 The Kitchen Garden
18 The Small Stables
19 The Large Stables
20 The Labyrinth

and grander palace on the site. The result was the Large Trianon, sometimes called the Marble Trianon because of the lavish use of colorful marble seen today. All of the marble was
quarried in France; the pink from Languedoc and the green
from the southern region near the Pyrenees Mountains. Like
most of Louis's building projects, he demanded that the Large
Trianon be massive in scale and as elaborately decorated as the
main palace itself.

But unlike the main palace of Versailles, the Large Trianon
is highly unorthodox in its shape. It consists of six long units
forming an asymmetrical series of connected galleries resembling dominos laid end-to-end at different right angles. The central architectural spine runs north-south roughly 650 feet, turns
at a right angle continuing in an east-west direction roughly another 450 feet, and then turns at another right angle heading
north-south for an additional 350 feet. The other three units,
each roughly 250 feet and parallel to one another, attach to the
first section of the central spine with a courtyard in between.
The total length, although approaching twenty-two hundred
feet, is still considerably smaller than the main palace itself.

The south wing of the Large Trianon was the location of
Louis's multiroomed apartment. Although not as large as those
in the main palace, it was nonetheless equally sumptuous. Before reaching the bedroom, the king first passed through three
antechambers. These richly decorated chambers were designed
to provide informal meeting rooms for small numbers of people.
Following these three rooms was the Mirrored Drawing Room,
used by Louis for his counsel chamber. In this room, Louis conducted official state meetings. Its name derives from the wide
use of alternating rectangular and arched mirror bays. Deep-
blue silk curtains adorned the room. The bedroom, used by
Louis as well as by several of his successors, had the bed against
one wall with a regal canopy above it. The walls, covered in a
deep-red fabric, created a majestic surrounding, complimented
by floors covered in highly stylized floral patterns.

Many modern architects and historians do not believe that
this palace expresses a concise, well-defined design. Historian
Guy Walton has this to say of the design:

> The Trianon is not, however, the brilliantly integrated
> and harmonious work sprung from the head of Mansart

that has often been suggested. The plan of the new Trianon is surprising at least, if not incoherent. Neither a château nor a palace, it is also no villa or casino. It has the elevation of an orangery, the plan of a warren and is made of the materials of a royal house. This confusion is brilliantly masked by the incontestable seductiveness of the place.

Under Louis XIV, the gardens of the Large Trianon, like those of the main palace, combined formal gardens that are highly geometric and precisely trimmed with the more open and thickly wooded parks decorated with waterfalls, water jets, and sculptures. The formal gardens were suited to viewing and the meandering of large groups of people, while the forested gardens were conducive to solitude and diversion from the formality of the court.

Initially built to provide Louis with refuge from the court, the Large Trianon quickly became a second palace for the nobility as well. Louis felt compelled to make a concession to their persistent presence to achieve the greater goal of keeping control over them.

PERISTYLES OF THE LARGE TRIANON

Louis closely watched the design of the Large Trianon. Letters between his architect, Mansart, and others provide historians with ample evidence that Louis played a major role in its design. The identifiable characteristics of this palace are the long galleries, the peristyles connecting the galleries, and the generous use of marble. Louis was so obsessed with a clean, orderly line to this structure that he banned the use of chimneys that extended above the visible roofline, even though doing so occasionally created smoky rooms within the buildings.

Louis demanded long peristyles, through which he could walk and enjoy the views of the formal gardens to the west. Peristyles are long, roofed corridors, open to the out-of-doors on one or both sides, intended for casual strolls and for connecting one building to another. First used by the Greeks and Romans to create shaded walkways to protect them from the oppressive hot Mediterranean sun, other cultures copied and used them for similar reasons. Those designed at Versailles allowed the nobility to wander in the shade during the summer and to remain dry

COURTLY NIGHT LIFE

At the Trianon palaces, many parties of various types took place, but only ladies were accorded the favor of privately dining with Louis, each having been carefully selected for a particular occasion. An invitation to dine with the king was not refused, although it often meant spending the night with the

Card games were often part of the lavish entertainment offered at the Trianon complex.

during the winter months. For Louis, the use of peristyles had the added bonus of providing dramatic views of his beloved gardens as he walked from one wing of the palace to another.

Mansart ornately decorated the peristyles of the Large Trianon beyond anything the Greeks or Romans could possibly have imagined. Being open to the elements, the materials had to be able to withstand the wind, sun, and rain. The floors, set with alternating black and white marble tiles, support the red marble columns and pilasters. The columns, positioned in sets of two, are of the Ionic style defined by the scrollwork carved on the capitals. The columns and pilasters support the ceilings, which are elegantly coffered with a design called alternating triglyphs and metopes, commonly found on the friezes of Greek and Roking. If a woman became a special favorite of the king, she might see her portrait hanging in a room called the Chamber of Beauties. Seventeen of these portraits have survived.

Large, lavish parties for hundreds were equally common. Entertainment relieved the boredom of life at Versailles and kept people from longing to be back at their own estates. The Marquis de Sourches, here quoted by Jean-Marie Pérouse de Montclos, records the following description of pleasures in his memoirs:

> Comedies were given three times a week, a ball every Saturday, and on the remaining three days all men and women of high rank gathered in the evening in the Grand Apartment of the king that was beautifully decorated with silver decorations worth more than six million *livres*. The suite was well lit and all guests were free to indulge themselves freely. One room had musicians who sang from time to time and an orchestra of woodwinds and violins playing music for those wishing to dance. In another room, the king and queen played card games on tables covered with beautiful embroidered tablecloths. Many servants were present who were at the complete disposal of the guests. In another room, the king played with the best players at the court on a billiard table. In yet another, a spectacular buffet for everyone wishing to eat and drink as much as they wished.

man buildings. A triglyph is a carved square panel designed to represent three vertical bars, usually followed by a carved square panel representing a sculptured form called a metope. These alternate along the length of the peristyle.

CONTROLLING THE COURT NOBILITY

Keeping all of the court nobility and their families under his control at Versailles on a full-time basis was a tricky proposition for Louis. Not only did he need to house, feed, and entertain them, even more importantly, he needed to mold and control their behavior at the court by devising ways of expressing his favor or disfavor. Writing at the time of Louis XIV, the court historian and gossip Saint-Simon records this phenomenon:

In this photo of the Large Trianon, the elaborate peristyles that Louis ordered can be clearly seen. The columns and pilasters that support the ceilings are elegantly carved.

Louis kept everyone around him attentive to his pleasure by offering frequent festival entertainment, private walks at Versailles, and trips about the countryside. All of these were tools that the king used to mark his favor or disfavor by naming those chosen to participate. He understood that he did not have at his disposal enough real favors to keep this activity in constant motion, realizing that he would need to substitute meaningless activities for the real ones. Playing upon court jealousy, Louis carefully distributed gestures of preference through the day, thus manifesting his considerable artfulness in such manners. No one was more ingenious than he in inventing small distinctions and associating great prestige to them.

Of all the favors Louis bestowed upon the nobility, none had greater significance than the assignment of apartments at the various palaces. The most desirable apartments were always those closest to the king's apartment. Generally larger and more elaborately decorated, they also were the ones with fireplaces and windows. The least desirable apartments, those occupying the southern wing of the main palace, could be wretched, very often having neither a fireplace nor window. A fall from royal favor usually meant banishment to a lesser apartment. When such an event took place, all the nobility at Versailles knew about it and gossiped about it. The constant threat of losing a desirable apartment kept them on their best behavior to avoid the same embarrassment. If someone gravely offended the king, he or she, along with family members, was banished from Versailles by Louis; a fate the nobility avoided at all costs.

THE KING'S FAVORS

After the granting of apartments, gaining access to the king was the most sought after privilege. This was one of the "meaningless activities" that Saint-Simon described in his *Mémoires*. When Louis retired in the evening, as many as 150 nobles gathered for the bedchamber ritual. He would announce in a strong voice the name of the distinguished man on whom he bestowed the honor of carrying the king's candlestick. Carrying the candlestick was a great honor, as was taking the candlestick back to one's own apartment for display as a trophy.

Louis had many rituals that he concocted to keep the nobles in line and loyal to him, including allowing privileged noblemen to carry the king's candlestick or to wear a special long jacket.

Another of the "meaningless activities" that excited the nobles was the awarding of a special long jacket. It was quite distinguished, lined in red with cuffs and embroidered with a magnificent design of gold and a bit of silver that was specific to this article of clothing. Among the few Louis allowed to wear it were members of his immediate family and princes directly related to him. The most distinguished members of the court begged the king to grant this favor either to themselves or to those close to them, and it was held to be a great honor to have received it. As soon as one became available, there was considerable jostling among the most privileged members of the court as to who would receive it next. If it went to a younger man, the honor was held to be especially great.

Life for the nobility became an endless succession of meaningless social rituals centered on honors bestowed by the king throughout his daily routines and during his pompous social activities. All the activities that at one time had purpose had now given way to purposelessness, governed by nothing more than etiquette. By granting all of these meaningless honors to the nobility, Louis gave them the satisfaction of thinking that they were participating in the administration of government. Louis, on the other hand, had the satisfaction of knowing that they were not.

VERSAILLES AFTER LOUIS XIV

Immediately upon the death of Louis XIV, the Duc d'Orléans exited the king's bedroom in the main palace to announce to the gathered royalty that the king had died. Following this proclamation, the Duc de Bouillon, with a black feather in his hat, announced in a loud voice to a crowd gathered below the king's balcony, "The king is dead." Replacing the black feather with a white one he pronounced, "Long live the king," in reference to the new king, Louis XV.

With this changing of the guard, the era of unrestrained building expansion at Versailles ended. Like many of his historic predecessors, whether Greek, Roman, or French, Louis XIV created an architectural statement that none of his successors could possibly surpass. For reasons of financial distress and lack of royal motivation, Versailles's future could no longer expect unlimited spending.

Born at Versailles in 1710, Louis XV, the great-grandson of Louis XIV, was only five when his great-grandfather died. Although born at Versailles, Louis XV did not inherit the commanding and flamboyant personality of his great-grandfather, nor did he possess his great-grandfather's interest in continuing the building tradition at Versailles.

LOUIS XV'S PLACE IN HISTORY

While Louis XV was a boy, his advisors kept him somewhat isolated, causing him to develop a secretive and remote personality that characterized his reign as king. Louis tended to prefer the solitude of private activities to the crowds of aristocratic partygoers that his predecessors enjoyed. During this early period, the nobility and the clergy again began running amok, creating domestic problems for the king. A failure to pay attention to the continuing conflict between the nobility and the peasantry was bringing this social division closer to the brink of violent conflict.

His advisors, who had moved him to Paris, recommended that he return to Versailles when he was twelve and that he marry as soon as possible to produce an heir to the throne. After Louis rejected a ten-year-old Spanish princess, court advisors prompted him to choose a Polish princess eight years his senior.

Viewed by most historians as a relatively inept king, Louis XV relied upon one advisor after another to chart the course of France's foreign policy throughout his fifty-nine-year reign between 1715 and 1774. During this period, the foreign policy of France involved three wars that saw France acquire some territory from Poland but, ultimately, lose far more foreign territory in North America to the English.

Louis XV's internal policy sought to address the inequality of the social classes and the inequity of the tax structure, but this progressive attitude died with Louis in 1774. During his reign France lost much of the hard-earned power and prestige his predecessors had acquired within the European community.

Louis XV, great-grandson of Louis XIV, became king when most boys begin attending kindergarten. Shyer than his predecessor, Louis XV was considered an ineffective monarch.

To assist the very young king in commanding France, Philippe II, Duc d'Orléans, governed in his place until 1723 when Louis turned thirteen. In 1726, Louis appointed André Hercule de Fleury as Prime Minister until Fleury's death seventeen years later. This was the only period of stability during Louis's reign. Louis XV, unlike his great-grandfather, avoided the responsibilities of governing whenever possible in favor of pursuing his interests in the natural sciences, especially his interest in establishing zoological and botanical gardens. He is sometimes quoted as having said that the arrival of the first pineapple at Versailles in 1751 was one the triumphs of his reign.

By the end of his lengthy reign, the future of France was markedly dimmer than it had been for generations. French historians often cited the most famous quotation attributed to Louis XV, "After me, the deluge," as a prophecy that would be fulfilled fourteen years later with the outbreak of the French Revolution. This historical event in 1789 began with the storming of the Bastille prison in nearby Paris, followed by the storming of Versailles by mobs of peasant farmers hungry to exact a terrible revenge for centuries of oppression.

LOUIS XV'S VERSAILLES

The young king passed his first seven years of life in Paris. During this absence from Versailles, the royal chambers were abandoned to visitors who wandered the empty rooms and hallways. Peter the Great, the tsar of Russia, while visiting Versailles during this time stayed in one of the royal apartments and had the audacity to demand that the groundskeepers turn on the fountains for his amusement.

Louis XV left behind only two significant additions to Versailles; the chapel located in the north wing of the main palace and the Petit or Small Trianon near the Large or Marble Trianon built by Louis XIV. Compared to the building program of Louis XIV, this represents an insignificant percentage of the total estate. Historians cite various explanations for this fact. The most obvious is that Louis XIV's exhaustive building program had severely depleted the finances of France. Another was the difference in personalities of the two kings. Louis XV was a more modest man than was his predecessor; preferring to pursue his interests in science than to enhance his regal international reputation. In addition to these two explanations, the French historian Jean-Marie Pérouse de Montclos suggests a third. Pérouse de Montclos believes that Louis XV's reluctance to continue the aggressive expansion of Versailles may in part be attributed to Louis XIV's deathbed advice to his great-grandson, "Do not emulate me in my taste for building and war."

THE OPERA HOUSE

The single most notable expansion at Versailles by Louis XV was the Opera House, located near the chapel on the north wing of the main palace. Envisioned but never executed by Louis XIV, initial designs were drawn up in 1765 by the architect Gabriel. It was completed five years later in 1771 to coincide with the marriage of Louis XVI and Marie-Antoinette of Austria.

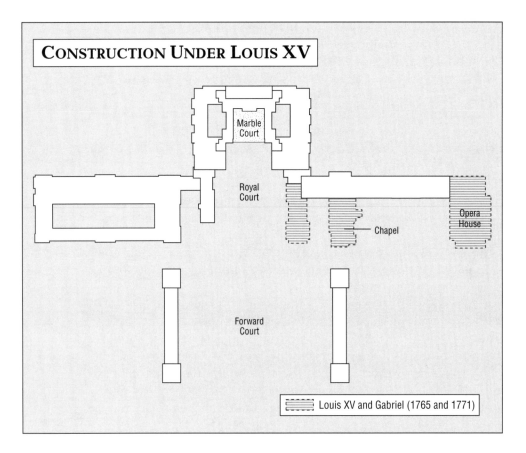

CONSTRUCTION UNDER LOUIS XV

Marble
Court

Royal
Court

Chapel

Opera
House

Forward
Court

Louis XV and Gabriel (1765 and 1771)

The oval shape of the Opera House was in keeping with Italian designs of the time to provide the best possible viewing for the theatergoers. No seat or private box had an obstructed view and the interior decorations were made of wood, whenever possible, for improved acoustics. The hand-carved wood was painted either in gold leaf, which created a dazzling effect in candlelight, or in an imitation marble. The main supports of the Opera House, however, were made of stone to reduce the possibility of fire in an enclosed theater, where escape for the spectators would be unlikely. Fire was always a serious consideration for architects of that era because the only means for illuminating such an auditorium was candlelight.

The designers placed private boxes along the perimeters of the second and third levels for the highest-ranking nobility. Traditionally, the highest row of private box seats, known as the Paradise Section, was reserved for the upper nobility, and the center-most of these belonged to the king. Louis XV, however, reluctant to show himself in public, chose to occupy a private box hidden by a grill so that operagoers could not see his face.

Famous opera composers of the time wrote for Louis XV, much to the continued appreciation of opera lovers. When not used for staging operas, a large wooden platform covered the orchestra pit, converting the entire theater into a grand ballroom for dancing and banquets.

This photograph of the interior of the Opera House reveals its rounded shape, tiers of private boxes, and dazzling gold-leafed woodwork.

SEVENTEENTH-CENTURY CONSTRUCTION TOOLS

The array of tools available to the builders of Versailles was remarkably similar to that available to their Egyptian, Greek, and Roman predecessors. Although several thousand years removed from their ancient ancestors, the implements available to the builders of Versailles had not significantly progressed beyond basic tools.

Most of the tools used to construct Versailles measured basic principles of physics. To ensure level floors, engineers used water levels to guarantee perfectly flat foundation trenches. As walls went up, engineers dropped plumb lines at the corners. These plumb lines were nothing more than a string with a weight dangling at one end. By hanging these from the corners of a room, builders knew whether the walls were perfectly straight or not on their vertical axis. Corners of rooms, designed to be at ninety degree right angles, were tested for accuracy with a square; two lengths of wood set precisely at a right angle to one another. Stone masons set-

THE PETIT OR SMALL TRIANON

Just as Louis XIV created the Porcelain Trianon and the Large Trianon to escape the crush of the nobility at the main palace, so too did Louis XV build the Small or Petit Trianon to escape that at the Large Trianon. Louis XV began construction on the Small Trianon in 1760 and completed it in 1764. Ostensibly built for his wife, Madame de Pompadour, she did not live long enough to see it completed. Therefore, the first person to occupy it was Marie-Antoinette, who accepted it as a gift from her husband, Louis XVI, the year of his coronation in 1774.

Significantly smaller than the Large Trianon, the Small Trianon is roughly a square one hundred feet on each side. Simple in design compared to the other two palaces, the Small Trianon consists of a basement, a main floor, and a small upper story. Many architects consider the Small Trianon and its gardens to be more interesting than the Large Trianon and its gardens. On the ground floor, the architects built the kitchens, guards' quarters, billiard room, and offices. The second floor consisted of the royal apartments, two dining rooms, and a library. Louis XV was so insistent on personal privacy that he did not even want the waiters to disturb the dining of his guests. To accomplish this

ting stone blocks and bricks were guided along perfectly straight lines by tightly fastening a string anchored from one corner of a building to the next corner.

Tools for cutting and carving stone were very similar in design to those used by the Greeks and Romans. These iron tools were harder and held their sharp edge longer than ancient ones, but their forms and uses were identical. Stonemasons used chisels of various sizes and shapes to cut and sculpt individual stones. Augers were used to drill holes into the stone when iron clamps were needed to hold the blocks together.

Carpenters, whose work focused primarily on building temporary wooden scaffolding and wooden floors, used hand tools familiar to ancient and modern carpenters alike. Most commonly employed were draw knives for smoothing wooden planks, hand saws, drills, hammers, and rulers. The nails used in construction were hand forged and had squared shanks.

engineering marvel, his architects designed the tables in the dining room on elevators operated by ropes, pulleys, and counterweights. Attendants lowered the tables to the kitchens on the first floor, where cooks loaded them with food and sent them back up to the delight of the guests.

Although much smaller than the gardens of the main palace, the gardens at the Small Trianon appear to have been just as luxurious. During the summer, gardeners planted ninety-six thousand plants and placed another two million potted plants in the earth. This extravagant use of pots allowed gardeners to remove and replant all of the flowers on a day's notice if the king wished to change the color of the landscape.

Just as the main palace of Versailles had begun as a retreat for Louis XIII and the Large Trianon as a retreat for Louis XIV, the Small Trianon became the retreat for Louis XV. The irony of all of these retreats is that no matter how many the kings built, they always built another to escape the congested life at the court.

LOUIS XVI'S PLACE IN HISTORY

Louis XVI, grandson of Louis XV, was born at Versailles in 1754 and ascended the throne in 1774 at the age of twenty. Tragically

The Petit Trianon, designed by Jacques-Ange Gabriel for Louis XV. Many consider the architecture of the building more interesting than that of the Large Trianon.

for him, the historical marks of his reign were the outbreak of the French Revolution on July 14, 1789, and his subsequent death at the blade of the guillotine in 1793.

Historians generally consider Louis XVI to have been a man of low intellect and of weak personal character, poorly trained to function effectively as the leader of France. Very much in keeping with many of his distant relatives, Louis XVI preferred hunting stags and wild boar in the great forests of France to focusing on the political changes taking place in Europe or the growing social problems of poverty and class conflict within France. Second only to hunting, he loved to eat and was known to consume enormous meals. At a single breakfast, he once ate six eggs in a cheese sauce, a pound of sliced ham, an entire chicken, and four lamb chops, all washed down with one and a half liters of wine.

For more than a century before the outbreak of the revolution, the economy of France had experienced periods of severe downturn. These occurred principally because of the many wars and poor management of internal finances. The nobility had unfairly taxed the peasant and merchant classes, creating economic hardships for those least able to pay, and had unfairly controlled most of the land, fomenting conflict between the upper and lower classes.

At the outset of the French Revolution, during the reign of Louis XVI, the damage done by Louis XIII, Louis XIV, and Louis XV had already taken its toll. Of these four kings, historians consider Louis XVI to be the one least responsible for the terrible social and economic conditions on the eve of the revolution. Louis XVI, to his credit, attempted some economic reforms, although they proved to be unsuccessful. As the financial crisis worsened, a call to reconvene an assembly made up of all segments of the population, called the Estates-General, became popular. In 1788, public sentiment forced Louis to call for elections. Once in session, the Estates-General took control of the government and on July 14, 1789, the symbolic beginning of the French Revolution occurred when Parisians seized a prison called the Bastille and released all the prisoners. Three months later, Parisian revolutionaries stormed the Versailles palace, forcing Louis and his

RENOVATION OF THE ROYAL APARTMENTS

In the interest of updating the apartments for greater comfort, Louis XV ordered the alteration of many of the smaller ones at the main palace. Newly introduced were small porcelain heaters to assist the larger wood-burning fireplaces and bells connected to ropes for summoning servants. Louis also introduced elevators to Versailles for raising and lowering food and other small items, in addition to those built to carry people. In 1772, one of the king's building supervisors invented Venetian blinds (so named because the designer was from Venice) to cover windows overlooking interior courts.

Interior decorations also underwent remodeling. Decorative woods and plaster were placed along the perimeters of the rooms. Wood or mirrored panels replaced fabric that at one time covered many of the walls in the more elegant rooms. These panels were far more ornate and richly embellished than any of the previous decorations. This new style of ornamental decorations, richly highlighted in lacquer paint, represented the beginnings of a style called Rococo that swept across all of Europe.

wife, Marie-Antoinette, to flee and live under arrest in Paris. In 1791, the French revolutionary army captured Louis and his family attempting to escape from France to Austria. Returned to Paris under armed guard, Louis and Marie-Antoinette swore their allegiance to the revolution (while secretly working against its objectives). Finally, on January 21, 1793, condemned to death by the National Convention, Louis and Marie-Antoinette died at the blade of the guillotine before a crowd of thousands who had gathered to watch their heads roll.

LOUIS XVI'S BUILDING AT VERSAILLES

Of all of the kings to occupy Versailles, Louis XVI experienced the shortest reign and pursued the most modest building program. Occupying Versailles as king for only fifteen years, Louis spent most of his energy coping with a depleted treasury resulting from the wars and fiscal mismanagement of his predecessors and from his own financing of the American Revolution. Opting to reform France's social and fiscal dilemmas, the only major building Louis had time for was a miniature model of a French village called the Hamlet.

THE HAMLET

Although Louis XVI was least responsible for France's dismal economic problems, he bore the brunt of the responsibility for the excesses of his ancestors.

Built for Louis XVI's queen, Marie-Antoinette, between 1783 and 1785, the Hamlet was intended to imitate a rustic peasant village. The Hamlet was, in effect, a private compound for the queen consisting of the types of simple buildings one might find in any one of hundreds of small rural villages scattered throughout eighteenth-century France. Designed by the architect R. Mique, it sits within the English gardens that replaced the botanical gardens built by Louis XV. Historians of this period regarded the Hamlet as the most charming setting in all of the nineteen-thousand-acre Versailles estate.

Reproducing a rustic village for the queen of France required an artistic touch that elevated it far above the realities of eighteenth-century peasant life. The visual focus of the Hamlet

Louis XVI steals a few moments with his beloved family before he is taken to be executed by the revolutionary mobs.

was the queen's house, set by a grassy garden that ran along the edge of a picturesque pond. Of the other buildings that have survived or partially survived, there exist a dairy barn, a billiards cottage, a reception cottage, a mill, complete with mill wheel that never actually operated, a cottage where food brought from one of the larger palaces could be reheated, and a tower that served only a decorative role.

Said to have been modeled after a village in the farming region of Normandy, along the western Atlantic coast, the buildings' exteriors are stucco, stone, and brick, held together by heavy timber support beams. The thatched roofs of the buildings elegantly carry over the architectural theme of peasant simplicity. The queen's cottage, the centerpiece of the Hamlet, has a wooden balustrade along the side facing the millpond with an elegant spiraling wooden staircase winding down to the grass garden below.

The Hamlet, built for Marie-Antoinette, resembled a rural town. When she visited the Hamlet, Marie-Antoinette often liked to pretend she was a simple peasant living a rustic life.

DECLINE AND DECAY

The flight of the royal couple from Versailles in 1789 ended this magnificent estate's function as the court of France. After more than a thousand years of autocratic rule on the part of the kings of France, the legendary grandeur of life at Versailles never resurfaced. As the king and queen departed their home, destined for the guillotine, this celebrated estate witnessed the scattering of nobles to the four corners of France, where many awaited the same fate as their king and queen.

No longer populated by the nobility, protected by guards, or maintained by millions of livres annually, Versailles quickly declined. The palace and gardens fell prey to the elements, thieves, and to the new revolutionary government in need of money.

In 1793, the revolutionary government ordered the sale of many of the châteaux throughout France to raise money but specifically exempted Versailles. This same revolutionary government did not, however, exempt the contents of Versailles, ordering the sale of 17,000 pieces of furniture at auction between August 23, 1793, and August 11, 1794.

The pillaging of art and the remaining furniture went on unabated until Napoleon Bonaparte came to power during the first decade of the eighteenth century, about fifteen years after Louis XVI and Marie-Antoinette fled Versailles. Almost any object not set in concrete was subject to theft, with works of art being the favorites. When Louis XIV became king, he inherited

MOCKING THE POOR

Many historians have taken the view that the creation of the Hamlet, a peasant village at Versailles for the favor of the queen of France, confirms the degree to which the ruling family had alienated itself from the common people. Simply stated, the Hamlet was a mockery and an insult to the peasants who lived their lives in poverty, subject to the inequality of the laws. Jean-Marie Pérouse de Montclos quotes François-Louis Poumiés de la Sibotie, a doctor traveling in France who visited Versailles, who made this comment about the Hamlet in his memoirs:

> Later I resolved to revisit Trianon, that place so dear to the unfortunate queen. I returned to the Small Trianon, to what was known as the Hamlet. This consists of a farm, a dairy, a parsonage, a mill, a master's house, a bailiff's house, an overseer's house, and finally the Marlborough Tower. On certain days the court gathered at Trianon, in the Hamlet. Louis XVI was master of the village, his two brothers were bailiff and schoolmaster, and the queen was the farmer's wife who preferred being in the dairy barn, the interior of which was completely covered in marble. Everyone wore peasant costumes. Louis enjoyed playing these games and did so with ease and a simplicity that was admirable. All of the thatched cottages had a rustic look, but their interiors were covered with elegant and luxurious marble.

150 paintings from his father. In 1710, the year of his death, he owned about twenty-three hundred, and by the time of the French Revolution, the number at Versailles had grown to about four thousand; all of which had disappeared as a result of either theft or auction.

Without the thousands of servants to repair and tend to the needs of the estate, buildings and gardens quickly fell into disrepair. Early nineteenth-century visitors wrote letters home

THE ROLE OF VERSAILLES IN THE FRENCH REVOLUTION

The role that Versailles played in the gathering storm of the French Revolution of 1789 is, to this day, a matter of continuous debate among historians of two differing points of view. One group sees the Versailles estate and its opulent lifestyle as the most significant cause of the French Revolution and the other sees Versailles, representing the leisure life of the nobility, as merely one of many causes.

Viewed as an isolated symbol of aristocratic excess, built by the taxes and labor of the peasantry and merchants, Versailles played a major role in the French Revolution. There can be no discounting the fact that Louis XIV and his successors poured extraordinary amounts of money into a building program and lifestyle benefiting only the wealthiest segment of the French population. One year alone, the amount of money spent on Versailles was equal to one half the total amount of money spent on the entire nation. This enormous symbol served to galvanize the antiroyalist sentiment that had been brewing for many generations.

Viewed as one of many causes of the French Revolution, Versailles's significance is diminished. Scholars of French history cite several causes of the revolution. Most obvious was the class conflict that had existed between the nobility and peasantry for generations that prevented the peasants from achieving equality of opportunity and equality under the law. Coupled with this class distinction was the problem of inequitable taxation. Neither the nobility nor the Catholic Church paid taxes, leaving the entire burden on the peasantry and the merchant class. In addition to taxation were the financial problems resulting from unsuccessful wars, loans to assist

telling of buckets in the palace hallways to capture water dripping through the roof. Vagabonds roamed the great marble hallways and grand ballrooms looking for places to sleep. Illustrators of the time sketched scenes of the gardens, depicting uprooted trees fallen across broken fountains that had once entertained the kings and their guests.

At the height of the revolution during the last decade of the eighteenth century, the hatred of the kings and nobility was so

the American Revolution, and several years of substandard crop production. Ironically, a final cause was the success of the American Revolution in 1776 that provided a philosophical basis for the peasants' demand to overthrow the nobility.

French peasants march to Versailles to storm the palace. During the French Revolution, the extravagant palace became a symbol for the excesses of the aristocracy.

intense that thoughts of protecting Versailles were viewed as unpatriotic. As the revolution took hold and the people of France recognized their democracy to be on sound footing, leaders came forward who acknowledged that Versailles might one day have value as an historic site.

RE-EMERGENCE AND RESTORATION

The end of the successful revolution at the beginning of the nineteenth century witnessed the re-emergence of France as a dominant member of the European community under the leadership of Napoleon Bonaparte (1769–1821). Napoleon and subsequent leaders of France recognized the value of maintaining Versailles as a national treasure. Napoleon, along with Louis XVIII (1755–1824) and Louis-Philippe (1773–1850), fantasized about using Versailles as their personal residence, but none did

Napoleon Bonaparte was the first French leader to see the value in restoring Versailles.

so, knowing that it would be an unpopular decision with the citizens of France. Instead, each of these rulers worked to restore Versailles to its previous reputation as France's foremost symbol of fame and grandeur.

Napoleon Bonaparte began the restoration project by ordering furniture makers to begin replenishing those lost treasures and by ordering the return to Versailles of all missing paintings.

Louis-Philippe, dubbed the Citizen King, who ruled France between 1830 and 1848, continued Napoleon's work by establishing the Museum of French History at Versailles. Opening it in 1837, Louis-Philippe dedicated the museum to collecting patriotic art that glorifies France. At that time, he oversaw the restoration of galleries and rooms containing more than four thousand paintings and portraits and one thousand works of sculpture.

Louis-Philippe set out to organize, catalog, and restore as much as possible. An undertaking of such magnitude required the conversion of many of the largest rooms in the palace to warehouses, cataloging rooms, and laboratories. Curators and chemists experimented with solvents, lacquers, varnishes, paints, and other chemicals used in the restoration process. For long periods, Versailles looked more like a laboratory than the palace of its past or the museum of its future. Gradually, curators began the restoration of the major rooms.

Between 1833 and 1834, King Louis-Philippe reconstructed the Gallery of Battles containing paintings of great military victories. Lining both sides of the gallery are paintings of thirty-two battles, beginning with the battle of Tolbiac in 1496 and ending with the battle of Wagram in 1809. Five paintings depict battles from the Napoleonic Wars.

VERSAILLES TODAY

Modern Versailles has been the recipient of generous grants of money from the French government, as well as from foreign philanthropists interested in preserving and restoring Versailles and its art. The most important development of the twentieth century has been the gradual transformation of the palace into a museum.

Not since the Parisians stormed Versailles on the eve of the French Revolution had the palace been the center of as much international attention as in 1919, the official end of World War I. Chosen as the site for the signing of the

King Louis-Philippe was one of the most dedicated and meticulous of the men who attempted to restore Versailles. He opened the Museum of French History at Versailles to inspire interest in preserving France's glorious past.

peace treaty ending the war, Versailles once again attracted international attention. Representatives from Europe and America joined in signing the treaty as the final ceremony of the war, with the great Hall of Mirrors serving as the backdrop.

Following the massive destruction of World War I, reconstruction at Versailles became a reality. The first period of modern restoration took place between 1925 and 1928 with the work being paid for by the Rockefeller Foundation. The Opera House received about $700,000 from the Rockefeller Foundation in 1925 and an additional $2,200,000 in 1928. This money, the most pledged up to that time, paid for many restoration projects. For

Crowds gather in the Hall of Mirrors to witness the signing of the Treaty of Versailles, which officially ended World War I.

the first time, basic work on interior woodwork began with sanding, repainting, and revarnishing.

World War II (1939–1945) interrupted the restoration, but by the early 1960s, several infusions of money, coupled with rising nationalism, pushed the restoration forward. In 1962, the Debré Decree required all Versailles furniture remaining in France in both public and private collecitons to be returned for public display.

Piece by piece and room by room, the palace curators returned the worn-out palace to its original splendor. Charles de Gaulle, then president of France, ordered the restoration of the Large Trianon in 1962 for use as an official residence for visiting dignitaries. As more and more tourists visited Versailles, additional funds were raised through entrance fees for the repair of the gardens and for the restoration of art and the king's and queen's apartments.

Today, visitors touring the estate at Versailles are treated to the same awe-inspiring elegance and beauty once reserved for kings and queens. The main rooms of the palace once again shimmer with the handcrafted wood carvings, the rich silk wall fabrics, the beautifully polished wood parquet floors, the sparkling crystal chandeliers, and the paintings and sculptures once enjoyed only by the nobility. The gardens are replanted and are as beautifully sculpted as when peasant gardeners worked there. Although most of the waterworks no longer spray their jets high into the air, the stone fountains and marble statuaries give the visitor the same view as that of the thousands of nobles who once traversed these paths on their daily walks.

A visitor today, witnessing this unparalleled estate, learns the history of France amid the babble of dozens of foreign languages representing many countries that did not exist at the time of Louis XIV and many others that did but were unknown to him. Versailles, once the home of the elite of France, is now open to all citizens of the world.

EPILOGUE

The story of Versailles is one of a rural village that grew to be the home of the most famous palace in Europe. Versailles began as a rustic agricultural village between Paris and the Normandy Peninsula during the sixteenth century at a time when its residents could never have imagined its final fame and majesty. Beginning as a simple hunting lodge built by King Louis XIII, it increased in size and majesty under the reign of Louis XIV to become the greatest palace ever built on the European continent.

The story of Versailles is predominately that of King Louis XIV. Other kings lived in the palace and enjoyed the pleasures of the gardens, but none left his mark as decisively as did Louis XIV. The estate of Versailles reflects the life of Louis XIV and his sense of his position in the world at that time. Ruling within the twin belief systems of absolutism and the divine right of kings, Louis spent more money, hired more workers, and demanded more of his architects, artists, and engineers than all of the other royal residents combined. Versailles is the result of his genius and energy.

THE NOBILITY'S PRISON AND THE KING'S ESCAPE

The story of Versailles is one of excess piled high atop excess. Of all the kings of Europe, Louis XIV was the supreme king. He built a palace and lifestyle admired and revered by all other kings. Not content with one enormous palace on his estate, he continued to build more. Boasting stables to accommodate his two thousand horses, a palatial structure to keep his orange trees warm, and canals large enough to accommodate gondolas, Louis's personal style became the standard for royal living throughout Europe. One year the total amount of money spent on various building projects at Versailles was equal to one half the total budget for the entire country. If Louis was not spending money on his passion for war, he was spending it on his passion for Versailles.

The story of Versailles is that of a prison. Although Louis never ordered the installation of steel bars or torture chambers, he nonetheless knew how to isolate nearly all of the French nobility in one place to keep them under his control. Before Louis XIV, the nobility had enjoyed a rich history of making most of the important political and economic decisions while the king held power in name alone. Louis XIV, a leader of unprecedented personal strength, developed a strong suspicion of the nobility. He determined that the best way of neutralizing their influence was to collect them in one place where he could keep them under his watchful eye. To accomplish this unusual objective, Louis required them to reside at Versailles so that he could determine what they could and could not do and where they could and could not go.

The story of Versailles is one of escape. Begun by Louis XIII as a hunting retreat, Versailles was expanded as an escape from Paris and the demands of France's nobility by Louis XIV. Having

The Hall of Mirrors was once the site of elegant dinners and parties for Versailles's residents. Louis XIV busied the nobility with social activities to keep them under his control.

Modern-day crowds at Versailles enjoy the grounds and the spectacular Neptune fountain. Contemporary visitors marvel at the excess and opulence of a bygone era.

rounded up the nobility and placed them under lock and key at the main palace at Versailles, Louis ironically created the need for yet another palace, the Large Trianon, to escape from their incessant demands. When too many nobles began to pressure him for dinner party invitations and gala fétes at the Large Trianon, Louis XV built yet another escape, the Small Trianon. As the kings of France rose to greater and greater heights, more and more of the nobility depended upon them for their government positions, their social status, and their entertainment. The more the kings controlled and manipulated the nobility, the more they felt the need to escape from them.

A CLASH OF EXTREMES

The story of Versailles is that of the very rich and the very poor living within the same estate. This was a place where tens of thousands of peasant workers occupying the lowest rung on the social ladder cared for the wealthiest families of France. The opulent and excessive lifestyle of the nobility conflicted with the abject poverty and misery of the poor. As the kings and nobles rose to greater and greater social and economic heights, they succeeded in distancing themselves from the very citizens they were obligated to protect and care for. In time, this distance caused resentment and open conflict between the privileged and the commoners. There is no historical evidence whatsoever suggesting that the kings living at Versailles realized that their alienation from the common people of France would in time lead to the French Revolution of 1789.

The story of Versailles is that of one of the most visited museums in the world. Each year, several hundred thousand visitors come to Versailles to learn of the kings who built it, to marvel at the artistry displayed in the art and architecture, and to stroll the beautifully preserved gardens. Each first-time modern visitor invariably asks the same questions: "How much did this cost?," "Who lived here?," and, "How could the nobility have lived in such extravagance while the peasants lived in such squalor?" Each visitor leaves Versailles with an enhanced understanding of the history of seventeenth- and eighteenth-century France, of the French Revolution, and of modern France.

GLOSSARY

architrave: The rectangular stone blocks that sit directly on top of the capital (top) of a column.

colonnade: A formal outdoor walkway flanked on each side by columns.

Corinthian style: The last of the three classical building styles, it is characterized by columns set on bases and elaborately carved capitals displaying acanthus leaves and other floral ornamentation.

coucher : The daily bedtime etiquette for the king, consisting of an elaborate ceremony during which honored members of the court attended to the needs of the king.

Doric style: The oldest of the three classical building styles, it is characterized by columns with no base and modestly carved capitals with very little ornamentation.

frieze: A decorative band of carved stone that runs the entire length of a building or peristyle.

Grand Couvert: The public dining ceremony permitting honored spectators to watch the king and queen eat dinner.

headers: A piece of heavy stone or wood beam that is set horizontally at the top of a window or door to support the weight above it.

Ionic style: The second of the three classical building styles, it is characterized by columns sitting on bases and carved capitals displaying a scroll motif.

lever: The daily morning etiquette for the king, consisting of an elaborate ceremony during which honored members of the court attended to his needs.

metope: A stone panel, plain or sculpted, set between the triglyphs on a frieze.

peristyle: A top-covered, open-sided colonnade surrounding a courtyard or connecting two buildings.

triglyph: A stone panel set between the metopes on a frieze, usually carved to represent three vertical bars.

For Further Reading

Charles Blitzer, *Age of Kings*. New York: Time Incorporated, 1967. This work provides the reader with a comprehensive discussion of the political climate in Europe during the seventeenth and eighteenth centuries. Blitzer discusses the politics of monarchy in the social context of the times and provides ample literary quotations supporting his conclusions about the origin, importance, and demise of monarchs.

James Farmer, *Versailles and the Court Under Louis XIV*. New York: The Century Company, 1905. Although written a long time ago, Farmer's book is a rich compendium of unusual information on the life at Versailles. Farmer cites Louis XIV's letters and historical documents of the period. This is a wonderful book full of esoteric historical data on the daily lives of Louis and his court.

Pierre-André Lablaude, *The Gardens of Versailles*. London: Zwemmer Publishers Limited, 1995. Of the many books on the gardens of Versailles, this one is one of the most comprehensive and readable. Generously laced with color photographs, Lablaude describes the layout of the gardens, waterworks, plantings, and the cost to build and maintain the vast gardens. Besides functioning as a wonderful history of the Versailles gardens, it is also a fascinating botanical discussion.

Nancy Mitford, *The Sun King*. New York: Harper & Row Publishers, 1966. Widely acclaimed as one of the great histories of the court at Versailles, Mitford's book focuses on the personalities at the court of Louis XIV. Written almost as a novel of intrigue and romance, the book includes gossip of the times and recounts the social events at Versailles.

Jean-Marie Pérouse de Montclos, *Versailles*. Paris: Abbeville Press, 1991. One of the most renowned architectural historians of France, Pérouse de Montclos has written a superb book chronicling the building of the Palace of Versailles along with all the secondary palaces and support buildings. This work walks the reader through the entire history of the estate from the time when it was merely a hunting lodge to its present life as a museum. Detailed architectural discus-

sions are richly complimented with superb color photographs.

Stephanie Pincas, *Versailles: The Story of the Gardens and Their
Sculpture.* New York: Thames and Hudson, 1996. Pincas
provides students interested in the Versailles gardens with
a lively history of the gardens and the art works within
them. She describes in detail the different types of gardens,
the designers who created them, and the history of land-
scaped architecture in France. She details the hundreds of
sculptures found in the gardens, their designers and their
connection with Greek and Roman themes.

WORKS CONSULTED

Joseph Bergen, *Cardinal Richelieu*. New Haven, CT: Yale University Press, 1985.

Robert W. Berger, *The Palace of the Sun—The Louvre of Louis XIV*. University Park: Pennsylvania State University Press, 1993.

———, *Versailles: The Château of Louis XIV*. University Park: Pennsylvania State University Press, 1985.

Alexander Dumas, *The Three Musketeers*. Trans. Lowell Blair. New York: Banton Books, 1984.

Ian Dunlop, *Versailles*. London: Hamish Hamilton, 1956.

Christopher Hibbert, *Versailles*. New York: Newsweek Book Division, 1972.

Jacques Levron, *Daily Life at Versailles in the Seventeenth Century*. London: George Allen and Unwin Ltd., 1968.

Elizabeth Worth Marvick, *Louis XIII—The Making of a King*. New Haven, CT: Yale University Press, 1986.

Duc de Saint-Simon, *Mémoires*. Paris: Borslisle, 1928.

Paul Sonnino, *The Reign of Louis XIV*. London: Humanities Press International, 1990.

Gerald Van der Kemp, *Versailles*. Paris: Vendome Press, 1978.

Guy Walton, *Louis XIV's Versailles*. Chicago: University of Chicago Press, 1986.

Gilette Ziegler, *At the Court of Versailles*. Trans. Simon Watson Taylor. New York: E.P. Dutton & Co., 1968.

INDEX

Picture Credits

Cover photos, clockwise from left: French Government Tourist Office, © Tony Stone Images/David Ball, Giraudon/Art Resource, NY

AKG London, 9, 14, 27, 34, 52, 74, 76

Corbis, 48

Corbis-Bettmann, 16, 20, 56, 69, 80, 86, 95

Foto Marburg/Art Resource, NY, 66

French Government Tourist Office, 11, 41, 58, 60, 99

Giraudon/Art Resource, NY, 31, 33, 38, 44, 83, 90

Edmond Lechevallier-Chevignard, *European Costumes of the Sixteenth Through Eighteenth Centuries*, Dover Publications, Inc., 1995, 12, 77

Michel Lemoine/Sipa Press, 100

Library of Congress, 25, 53, 94

National Archives, 96

North Wind Picture Archives, 88, 93

PhotoDisc, 64

Prints Old & Rare, 89

Scala/Art Resource, NY, 23

Rasmussen Soren/Sipa Press, 61

Baldwin H. Ward/Corbis-Bettmann, 22

About the Author

James Barter completed his undergraduate studies in history and classics at the University of California (Berkeley) followed by graduate studies in ancient history and archaeology at the University of Pennsylvania. Mr. Barter has taught history as well as Latin and Greek.

A Fulbright scholar at the American Academy in Rome, he worked on archaeological sites in and around the city. He also attended the Sorbonne University in Paris, making frequent visits to Versailles.

Mr. Barter lives in San Diego with his twelve-year-old daughter, Kalista, whose name in Greek means "most beautiful." His older daughter, Tiffany, is a violinist with the Virginia Symphony. Mr. Barter is well known for his slide presentations at local universities, bookstores, and museums.